Lecture Notes in Computer Science   12407

More information about this series at http://www.springer.com/series/7409

Ajay Katangur · Shih-Chun Lin ·
Jinpeng Wei · Shuhui Yang ·
Liang-Jie Zhang (Eds.)

Edge Computing – EDGE 2020

4th International Conference
Held as Part of the Services Conference Federation, SCF 2020
Honolulu, HI, USA, September 18–20, 2020
Proceedings

 Springer

Editors
Ajay Katangur
Missouri State University
Springfield, IL, USA

Jinpeng Wei (iD)
Department of Software
and Information System
University of North Carolina
Charlotte, NC, USA

Liang-Jie Zhang (iD)
Kingdee International Software
Group Co., Ltd.
Shenzhen, China

Shih-Chun Lin
North Carolina State University
Raleigh, NC, USA

Shuhui Yang
Purdue University Northwest
Hammond, IN, USA

ISSN 0302-9743   ISSN 1611-3349   (electronic)
Lecture Notes in Computer Science
ISBN 978-3-030-59823-5   ISBN 978-3-030-59824-2   (eBook)
https://doi.org/10.1007/978-3-030-59824-2

LNCS Sublibrary: SL3 – Information Systems and Applications, incl. Internet/Web, and HCI

This Springer imprint is published by the registered company Springer Nature Switzerland AG
The registered company address is: Gewerbestrasse 11, 6330 Cham, Switzerland

Preface

The International Conference on Edge Computing (EDGE) aims to become a prime international forum for both researchers and industry practitioners to exchange the latest fundamental advances in the state of the art and practice of edge computing, identifying emerging research topic, and defining the future of edge computing.

EDGE 2020 is a member of the Services Conference Federation (SCF). SCF 2020 had the following 10 collocated service-oriented sister conferences: the International Conference on Web Services (ICWS 2020), the International Conference on Cloud Computing (CLOUD 2020), the International Conference on Services Computing (SCC 2020), the International Conference on Big Data (BigData 2020), the International Conference on AI & Mobile Services (AIMS 2020), the World Congress on Services (SERVICES 2020), the International Conference on Internet of Things (ICIOT 2020), the International Conference on Cognitive Computing (ICCC 2020), the International Conference on Edge Computing (EDGE 2020), and the International Conference on Blockchain (ICBC 2020). As the founding member of SCF, the First International Conference on Web Services (ICWS 2003) was held in June 2003 in Las Vegas, USA. Meanwhile, the First International Conference on Web Services - Europe 2003 (ICWS-Europe 2003) was held in Germany in October 2003. ICWS-Europe 2003 was an extended event of ICWS 2003, and held in Europe. In 2004, ICWS-Europe was changed to the European Conference on Web Services (ECOWS), which was held in Erfurt, Germany.

This volume presents the accepted papers for the International Conference on Edge Computing (EDGE 2020), held virtually during September 18–20, 2020. EDGE 2020 focuses on the state of the art and practice of edge computing, in which topics cover localized resource sharing and connections with the cloud. We accepted 10 papers for these proceedings. Each was reviewed and selected by at least three independent members of the EDGE 2020 International Program Committee. We are pleased to thank the authors whose submissions and participation made this conference possible. We also want to express our thanks to the Organizing Committee and Program Committee members, for their dedication in helping to organize the conference and reviewing the submissions. Thank you to the volunteers, authors, and conference participants for the great contributions to the fast-growing worldwide services innovations community.

July 2020

Ajay Katangur
Shih-Chun Lin
Jinpeng Wei
Shuhui Yang
Liang-Jie Zhang

The original version of the book was revised: the affiliation of the second editor was not correct. This has now been rectified. The correction to the book is available at https://doi.org/10.1007/978-3-030-59824-2_11

Organization

General Chair

Karolj Sakla   Ruđer Bošković Institute, Croatia

Program Chairs

Ajay Katangur   Missouri State University, USA
Shih-Chun Lin   North Carolina State University, USA
Jinpeng Wei (Vice-chair)   College of Computing and Informatics, USA
Shuhui Yang (Vice-chair)   Purdue University, USA

Services Conference Federation (SCF 2020)

General Chairs

Yi Pan   Georgia State University, USA
Samee U. Khan   North Dakota State University, USA
Wu Chou   Vice President of Artificial Intelligence & Software
                                   at Essenlix Corporation, USA
Ali Arsanjani   Amazon Web Services (AWS), USA

Program Chair

Liang-Jie Zhang   Kingdee International Software Group Co., Ltd, China

Industry Track Chair

Siva Kantamneni   Principal/Partner at Deloitte Consulting, USA

CFO

Min Luo   Georgia Tech, USA

Industry Exhibit and International Affairs Chair

Zhixiong Chen   Mercy College, USA

Operations Committee

Jing Zeng   Yundee Intelligence Co., Ltd, China
Yishuang Ning   Tsinghua University, China
Sheng He   Tsinghua University, China
Yang Liu   Tsinghua University, China

Steering Committee

Calton Pu (Co-chair)	Georgia Tech, USA
Liang-Jie Zhang (Co-chair)	Kingdee International Software Group Co., Ltd, China

EDGE 2020 Program Committee

Maria Gorlatova	Duke University, USA
Mohammadreza Hoseinyfarahabady	The University of Sydney, Australia
Wei Li	The University of Sydney, Australia
Rui André Oliveira	University of Lisbon, Portugal
Ju Ren	Central South University, China
Weichao Wang	University of North Carolina at Charlotte, USA
Hung-Yu Wei	National Taiwan University, Taiwan
Mengjun Xie	The University of Tennessee at Chattanooga, USA

Conference Sponsor – Services Society

Services Society (S2) is a nonprofit professional organization that has been created to promote worldwide research and technical collaboration in services innovation among academia and industrial professionals. Its members are volunteers from industry and academia with common interests. S2 is registered in the USA as a "501(c) organization," which means that it is an American tax-exempt nonprofit organization. S2 collaborates with other professional organizations to sponsor or co-sponsor conferences and to promote an effective services curriculum in colleges and universities. The S2 initiates and promotes a "Services University" program worldwide to bridge the gap between industrial needs and university instruction.

The services sector accounted for 79.5% of the USA's GDP in 2016. The world's most service-oriented economy, with services sectors accounting for more than 90% of the GDP. S2 has formed 10 Special Interest Groups (SIGs) to support technology and domain specific professional activities:

- Special Interest Group on Web Services (SIG-WS)
- Special Interest Group on Services Computing (SIG-SC)
- Special Interest Group on Services Industry (SIG-SI)
- Special Interest Group on Big Data (SIG-BD)
- Special Interest Group on Cloud Computing (SIG-CLOUD)
- Special Interest Group on Artificial Intelligence (SIG-AI)
- Special Interest Group on Edge Computing (SIG-EC)
- Special Interest Group on Cognitive Computing (SIG-CC)
- Special Interest Group on Blockchain (SIG-BC)
- Special Interest Group on Internet of Things (SIG-IOT)

About the Services Conference Federation (SCF)

As the founding member of the Services Conference Federation (SCF), the First International Conference on Web Services (ICWS 2003) was held in June 2003 in Las Vegas, USA. Meanwhile, the First International Conference on Web Services - Europe 2003 (ICWS-Europe 2003) was held in Germany in October 2003. ICWS-Europe 2003 was an extended event of ICWS 2003, and held in Europe. In 2004, ICWS-Europe was changed to the European Conference on Web Services (ECOWS), which was held in Erfurt, Germany. SCF 2019 was held successfully in San Diego, USA. To celebrate its 18th birthday, SCF 2020 was held virtually during September 18–20, 2020.

In the past 17 years, the ICWS community has expanded from Web engineering innovations to scientific research for the whole services industry. The service delivery platforms have been expanded to mobile platforms, Internet of Things (IoT), cloud computing, and edge computing. The services ecosystem is gradually enabled, value added, and intelligence embedded through enabling technologies such as big data, artificial intelligence (AI), and cognitive computing. In the coming years, all the transactions with multiple parties involved will be transformed to blockchain.

Based on the technology trends and best practices in the field, SCF will continue serving as the conference umbrella's code name for all service-related conferences. SCF 2020 defines the future of New ABCDE (AI, Blockchain, Cloud, big Data, Everything is connected), which enable IoT and enter the 5G for the Services Era. SCF 2020's 10 collocated theme topic conferences all center around "services," while each focusing on exploring different themes (web-based services, cloud-based services, big data-based services, services innovation lifecycle, AI-driven ubiquitous services, blockchain driven trust service-ecosystems, industry-specific services and applications, and emerging service-oriented technologies). SCF includes 10 service-oriented conferences: ICWS, CLOUD, SCC, BigData Congress, AIMS, SERVICES, ICIOT, EDGE, ICCC, and ICBC. The SCF 2020 members are listed as follows:

[1] The International Conference on Web Services (ICWS 2020, http://icws.org/) is the flagship theme-topic conference for Web-based services, featuring Web services modeling, development, publishing, discovery, composition, testing, adaptation, delivery, as well as the latest API standards.

[2] The International Conference on Cloud Computing (CLOUD 2020, http://thecloudcomputing.org/) is the flagship theme-topic conference for modeling, developing, publishing, monitoring, managing, delivering XaaS (Everything as a Service) in the context of various types of cloud environments.

[3] The International Conference on Big Data (BigData 2020, http://bigdatacongress.org/) is the emerging theme-topic conference for the scientific and engineering innovations of big data.

[4] The International Conference on Services Computing (SCC 2020, http://thescc.org/) is the flagship theme-topic conference for services innovation lifecycle that includes enterprise modeling, business consulting, solution creation, services

orchestration, services optimization, services management, services marketing, and business process integration and management.

[5] The International Conference on AI & Mobile Services (AIMS 2020, http://ai1000.org/) is the emerging theme-topic conference for the science and technology of AI, and the development, publication, discovery, orchestration, invocation, testing, delivery, and certification of AI-enabled services and mobile applications.

[6] The World Congress on Services (SERVICES 2020, http://servicescongress.org/) focuses on emerging service-oriented technologies and the industry-specific services and solutions.

[7] The International Conference on Cognitive Computing (ICCC 2020, http://thecognitivecomputing.org/) focuses on the Sensing Intelligence (SI) as a Service (SIaaS) which makes systems listen, speak, see, smell, taste, understand, interact, and walk in the context of scientific research and engineering solutions.

[8] The International Conference on Internet of Things (ICIOT 2020, http://iciot.org/) focuses on the creation of IoT technologies and development of IoT services.

[9] The International Conference on Edge Computing (EDGE 2020, http://theedgecomputing.org/) focuses on the state of the art and practice of edge computing including but not limited to localized resource sharing, connections with the cloud, and 5G devices and applications.

[10] The International Conference on Blockchain (ICBC 2020, http://blockchain1000.org/) concentrates on blockchain-based services and enabling technologies.

Some highlights of SCF 2020 are shown below:

- **Bigger Platform:** The 10 collocated conferences (SCF 2020) are sponsored by the Services Society (S2) which is the world-leading nonprofit organization (501 c(3)) dedicated to serving more than 30,000 worldwide services computing researchers and practitioners. Bigger platform means bigger opportunities to all volunteers, authors, and participants. Meanwhile, Springer sponsors the Best Paper Awards and other professional activities. All the 10 conference proceedings of SCF 2020 have been published by Springer and indexed in ISI Conference Proceedings Citation Index (included in Web of Science), Engineering Index EI (Compendex and Inspec databases), DBLP, Google Scholar, IO-Port, MathSciNet, Scopus, and ZBlMath.
- **Brighter Future:** While celebrating the 2020 version of ICWS, SCF 2020 highlights the Third International Conference on Blockchain (ICBC 2020) to build the fundamental infrastructure for enabling secure and trusted service ecosystems. It will also lead our community members to create their own brighter future.
- **Better Model:** SCF 2020 continues to leverage the invented Conference Blockchain Model (CBM) to innovate the organizing practices for all the 10 theme conferences.

Contents

IoT Digital Forensics Readiness in the Edge: A Roadmap for Acquiring Digital Evidences from Intelligent Smart Applications

Andrii Shalaginov[1]([✉]), Asif Iqbal[2], and Johannes Olegård[2]

[1] Norwegian University of Science and Technology, Gjøvik, Norway
andrii.shalaginov@ntnu.no
[2] KTH Royal Institute of Technology, Stockholm, Sweden
asif.iqbal@ee.kth.se, jolegard@kth.se

Abstract. Entering the era of the Internet of Things, the traditional Computer Forensics is no longer as trivial as decades ago with a rather limited pool of possible computer components. It has been demonstrated recently how the complexity and advancement of IoT are being used by malicious actors attack digital and physical infrastructures and systems. The investigative methodology, therefore, faces multiple challenges related to the fact that billions of interconnected devices generate tiny pieces of data that easily comprehend the Big Data paradigm. As a result, Computer Forensics is no longer a simple methodology of the straightforward process. In this paper, we study the complexity and readiness of community-accepted devices in a smart application towards assistance in criminal investigations. In particular, we present a clear methodology and involved tools related to Smart Applications. Relevant artefacts are discussed and analysed using the prism of the Digital Forensics Process. This research contributes towards increased awareness of the IoT Forensics in the Edge, corresponding challenges and opportunities.

1 Introduction

Internet of Things (IoT) has brought virtually unlimited possibilities for the development of smart applications that target everyday's life improvement. With broadening horizons of such architecture's flexibility and automation, one can create a nearly autonomous system on private, corporate and national scales. While, undoubtedly, it is a positive development, there are few growing concerns from the perspective of security and safety. Diversity of used technologies a novel cyber threat landscape with a high chance of zero-day vulnerabilities and novel attack scenarios (e.g., Mirai botnet [4,15]). Moreover, it creates new challenges as well as opportunities for Crime Investigations involving the IoT ecosystem.

Despite the fact that each individual IoT Edge device is generally simpler than laptops or large-scale servers, there exist multiple limitations and challenges. Speaking of Digital Forensics Process [9,13,18], *Identification* phase

A. Katangur et al. (Eds.): EDGE 2020, LNCS 12407, pp. 1–17, 2020.
https://doi.org/10.1007/978-3-030-59824-2_1

might hit the wall when trying to identify the relevant information, where it stored originally in the IoT ecosystem and to whom it belongs, *Preservation* of the data might not be easy due to the fact that pieces of data are spread across multiple instances that do not relate to timestamps or data custodians in explicit ways, *Aggregation* of multiple pieces of data can easily end up being Big Data paradigm with the relevance and "needle in a haystack" issue, *Analysis* can yield irrelevant results, result from the lack of understanding of used IoT ecosystem, legally-binding agreement and personal data protection regulations. Finally, Smart Applications might introduce a layer of Machine Learning (ML) / Artificial Intelligence (AI) models, which require knowledge expert to interpret, possibly reverse-engineer and provide explainable answers on why the data have been processed and the automated decision been made [26, 27].

Unlike other research papers in the area, this contribution seeks an understanding of the forensics readiness of interconnected devices in the Edge, rather than of a stand-alone device. The focus is on the open-source platforms to create a corresponding road map for the investigative process along with recommendations. In particular, it was (i) created a Smart Application (environment sensors control) scenario with Edge devices involving IoT hub (Raspberry Pi) and IoT end-point devices (Arduino Uno and ESP8266), (ii) performed step-by-step collection of the artefacts in accordance to Digital Forensics Process and (iii) analysis of the acquired digital evidences from interconnected Edge devices using open-source existing tools. Finally, a special focus will be given to understanding and reverse-engineering ML/AI software found along with raw data on IoT devices' storage, considering omnipresence of such software in IoT appliances. The paper is organized as follows. The Sect. 2 presents an overview of the IoT forensics approaches and known artefacts that can be found across various types of devices. Further, Sect. 3 gives an overview of the suggested use case and particular methodological steps on Edge devices, while Sect. 4 included results of the Digital Forensics Process steps with corresponding artefacts from Smart Applications. Finally, Sects. 5 and 6 discusses IoT forensics readiness and overall preparedness of the Edge ecosystem for investigations.

2   Related Works

Due to widespread demand, cheap hardware, large community support and available plug-in components, the amount of IoT devices is growing exponentially, reaching 18 bln devices by 2022 according to Ericsson market study [8]. Out of those, 16 bln devices will be attributed to short-range devices. It means that rapid development of 4G+ (and 5G) connectivity and low-power wide range communication protocols (BLE - Bluetooth Low Energy, LoRa, IQRF and Zig-Bee) make geographically distributed communication very easy both in economic sense and deployment costs [22]. Therefore, it is important to keep in mind that IoT forensics is not only device-focused investigation, yet rather network- and cloud-oriented, as in the case with Edge devices.

"*Edge devices*" or "*Edge computing*" transformed the way how the data are handled in the distributed sensors networks. This technology brought disruption into data processing in a way that the data can be processed in the network while being transmitted from end-node IoT devices to data processing hubs and *"data lakes"* [24]. With all possible open-source platforms, sensors and actuators, the Edge devices are placed on the crossroads of all data streams flowing up and down the IoT ecosystem. The data that is transmitted and processed are ranging from the trivial regular (M2M) communication containing sensor measurements to user-related sensitive data containing credentials and personal information [23].

2.1 IoT Forensics: State of the Art

It is important to understand that the requirements for Digital Forensics methodologies that were used in the 1990s or even 1980s were completely different from what they are now, i.e. completely different from what is required in 2020s [20]. It is mainly due to the fact that cheap and easy-to-use technologies made it possible to generate an extreme amount of data, creating a paradigm of so-called Big Data. The amount of data will be grown bringing more challenges to police investigating cases, leaving the only way out is to adopt new technologies capable of processing and extracting real-world data.

Digital Forensics over the course of last decade became multi-faceted science targeting all possible aspects of discovering digital traces in a large set of data found at or attributed to a crime scene [17]. Speaking of Smart Applications from the infrastructure level, we can say that there are multiple components, resembling general IoT ecosystem: *Cloud data storage, IoT gateways, IoT nodes, sensors* and *actuators* dealing with tasks such as *data acquisition, aggregation, processing, analysis* and *data-driven decision making* [6]. Moreover, it is important to understand the challenges in Digital Forensics related to such versatile, multi-platform and cross-domain infrastructure. There are considerable differences in the computational and data processing capabilities of both IoT nodes, also called micro-controllers (Micro Controller Units, or MCU) and IoT gateways, also called micro-computers (System on a Chip, or SoC). Even though the size of the stored data is relatively small on each device, it can easily enter the Big Data paradigm once the Smart infrastructure has multiple nodes in the network. In addition, IoT brings challenges to digital pieces of evidence preservation attributed to boundary-less networks distributed over large regions. Therefore, *1-2-3 zone model* [18] of digital forensics investigation was suggested and covers all digital data found in fog, cloud, routers and gateway servers. This model differentiates between internal, middle and outer networks, however, still being complex. To facilitate flexibility, there was suggested a paradigm of "Fragile Evidence Zone" and [19] as a prerequisite for the data accumulation platform.

2.2 IoT Forensics: Order of Volatility and Data Preservation

Edge Computing is the intrinsically agile environment and most of the data can be considered as dynamic, bringing more constraints on the data identification and collection during digital forensics process. From the perspective of Digital Forensics, this can be a challenge due to the fact that the Order of Volatility needs to be maintained in a general way: Random Access Memory (RAM), network traffic, disk storage, etc [5]. However, one of the difficulties is related to the fact that the size of the storage in the Edge devices makes it impossible to store all the data. Therefore, only a few data pieces can be stored for a longer period, while others are gone. Another difficulty is that the crucial for forensics *"timestamps"* are not available on the devices like micro-controllers due to limited computational and storage capacity [14]. Even though, there exist timekeeping functionalities like Time Library for Arduino,[1] those do not commonly use to avoid unnecessary delays and computing overhead. As a result, the timestamps might be inevitably lost even if the files exist. At the same time, micro-computer platforms like Orange Pi or Raspberry Pi provide full support to maintain current and updated in a real-time manned time and data, leaving IoT gateway/hub tiers as the last with reasonably trustworthy timestamps. The amount of data available in each component differs a lot: from 32 KB of flash and 2 KB of RAM (Arduino) to 256 GB of SD card and 4 GB of RAM (Raspberry Pi). To the authors knowledge, there have not been explored enough analysis of digital pieces of evidence in a set of Smart Applications in Edge with respect to different types of memory defined in order of volatility. One of the community-accepted tools that can be used on microcomputers to facilitate the preservation of Order of volatility is "Forensics Mode" in Kali Linux.[2]

3   Use Case and Methodology

The main goal of this paper is to demonstrate possible ways of extracting relevant digital pieces of evidence from MCU and SoC devices found in the Edge. There will be given a general road map for such data acquisition on Smart Applications in the Edge, also taking in mind that ML / AI is one of the intelligent components of such an interconnected network. The peculiarity of DF in Smart Applications that we want to specifically highlight in this paper is the presence of intelligent models that were trained from the data. Currently, there exist a large number of intelligent ML models that can be used for *clustering, classification and* [16] such as *Artificial Neural Network (ANN), Support Vector Machines (SVM), Bayesian Network (BN), Hidden Markov Models (HMM)*. Technically speaking, ML can be trained from any kind of real-world data to be able to give a prediction regarding new previously unseen data sample. Moreover, according to Deloitte [25], 80% of enterprise IoT solutions will include ML/AI components. Therefore, this section presents the way how ML models can be used in the Smart Application and how those can be integrated into the DF process as a *digital evidence*.

3.1   Smart Applications: Edge Devices

A scenario that we tailored is smart application closed-loop controller (IoT hub) that handles communication with IoT end-node devices harvesting

---

[1] https://playground.arduino.cc/Code/Time/.

[2] https://docs.kali.org/general-use/kali-linux-forensics-mode.

environmental parameters such as temperature and humidity. Such scenario generally consist of the following components on a high level: *sensor* - a simple passive circuit that "senses" physical world measurements and converts to electrical signal, *controller* - devices that make decision based on the input sensor measurements and *actuator* - a simple active device that can do physical actions upon controlling electrical signal. This interconnected network also provides a *feedback loop*, while actuator performing actions based on the measurements from sensors [7]. Basic communication in such scenarios is usually organized via Message Queuing Telemetry Transport (MQTT) protocol as a lightweight and reliable solution for transmission of sensor data and actuators commands. An example of Smart Application-based systems is shown in the Fig. 1.

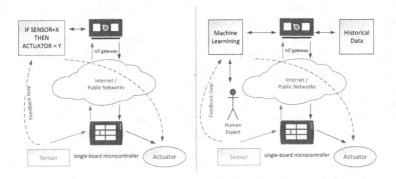

Fig. 1. Regular rule-based (*left*) and intelligent Machine Learning-based (*right*) implementation of the feedback loop in Smart Applications

3.2   Experimental Environment

For the demonstration purpose, we model a core architecture of the *Smart Home*, also found in other domains - intelligent monitoring with a *feedback loop*. An imaginary scenario was developed (inspired by [28]), where the IoT node uses the ML model trained on the IoT gateway to protect against cyber attacks. The diagram of the experimental installation shown in the Fig. 2. As mentioned earlier, this includes the following components with computational capabilities:

IoT hub/gateway is implemented using *Raspberry Pi 3 Model B* (1.2 GHz Quad-Core CPU, 1 GB RAM, 16 GB MicroSD card, Ethernet). It is one of the most lightweight and low-end SoC with minimal system components required to run OS. It has Raspbian 4.19 (Debian Buster 4.19) installed. To demonstrate also intelligent application, we have ported *ArduinoANN* project[3] from AVR to ARM to specifically simulate ANN training step using Mosquittopp v.1.5.7-1 (MQTT version 3.1/3.1.1 client C++ library and corresponding Broker), Boost v.1.67.0-13 for uBLAS vector storage and JSON serialization, g++ v. 4:8.3.0-1

---

[3] http://robotics.hobbizine.com/arduinoann.html.

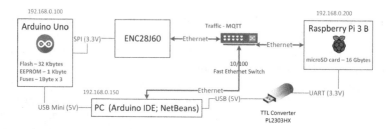

Fig. 2. Experimental setup used in this paper, including IoT node and IoT gateway. Types of the media with corresponding size are denoted in *red font*

as a compiler. This node was assigned IP address 192.168.0.200. SoC needs a reliable power supply and, in some cases, can run from the battery.

IoT node is implemented using *Arduino Uno rev. 3* (16 MHz CPU, 2 KB RAM, 32 KB, ENC28J60 Ethernet board). ArduinoIDE 1.8.9 was used to program Arduino UNO. The communication protocol implementation was done using the following libraries: UIPEthernet 2.0.7 to work with ENC28J60 Ethernet controller, PubSubClient 2.7.0 and ArduinoJson 6.11.5, while the testing phase was inspired by *ArduinoANN* project. To reduce the size of the code and accommodate larger packers, the configuration of the first and second libraries were changed to UID_CONF_UDP_CONNS = 1 and MQTT_MAX_PACKET_SIZE = 256 respectively. This node was assigned to address 192.168.0.100. It was used Ethernet protocol instead of WiFi on Arduino to set up the baseline. It has faster initialization, lower price and simpler connection routine for the experiment phase. MCU can easily run from battery or solar power.

Stand-alone IoT device without ML. To contrast the rest of the paper, we will study a stand-alone IoT device that does not use ML. The diagram of the experimental installation shown in the Fig. 3. The device is connected to a WiFi network and sends data directly (i.e. without an intermediate edge-device) to a remote server. The device has a ESP32-WROOM-32D [10] (2.4 GHz and 520 KiB RAM) processor and a 16 MiB flash memory. It does not run a full operating system. This makes the device more powerful than the Arduino and but less powerful than the raspberry pi. It behaves like a MCU but has capabilities closer to a SoC. The device is used to measure temperature and humidity. The device has an Universal Asynchronous Receiver/Transmitter (UART) interface.

3.3 Digital Forensics Process in the Internet of Things

IoT Digital Forensics is a relatively new field were two important issues have to be counted in: *firstly*, limited computational capabilities does not allow to implement security mechanisms exposing more data to forensics investigators, *secondly*, previously unseen and undocumented proprietary technologies will delay data analysis requiring an additional level of reverse-engineering. Due to connectivity and versatility of the devices, it becomes a real challenge to fix the baseline

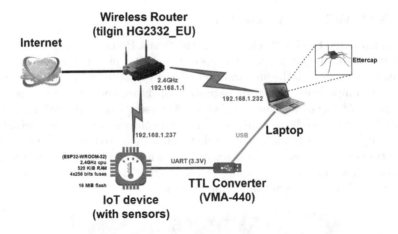

Fig. 3. Experimental setup for the stand-alone IoT device without ML

in the so-called Digital Forensics process [12]. Despite the lack of standardization, improper pieces of evidence handing and challenging chain of custody in IoT ecosystem, the authors emphasized that *pre-investigation readiness* and *real-time integration* will be a key to successful digital forensics investigation in IoT in future [31]. From the perspective of the Digital Forensics, there can be highlighted multiple phases suggested over the last decades [30]. However, from the approach strategy, one needs to define the following stages:

Field Work and Acquisition. This stage includes *Identification, Preservation and Collection* of the Smart Devices from the crime scene, identifying their relevance and storing according to predefined Chain of Custody.

Lab Work and Analysis. During this stage *Examination, Analysis and Presentation* are performed, when a Forensics Investigator extracted data from Smart Devices and tries to link them together attributing found pieces of evidence to a crime scene.

4   Computer Forensics Investigation in the Edge

This section will explain step-by-step digital pieces of evidence analysis and roadmap for extracting data in the Edge. As was mentioned before, we emphasize the importance of understanding how the ML models work and their particular place in the IoT. While speaking about IoT, there can be seen three following areas where data normally exist: *cloud, network and devices*, while IoT digital forensics readiness is still a challenge as explained by Alenezi et al. [3]. Particularly, there is a need to maintain log files, transmit relevant data and store timestamps, that might require modification of the IoT infrastructure. Therefore, we will be going step by step in this section over the approaches to acquire and then analyze any relevant data from Smart Applications.

4.1 Field Work and Acquisition

As also mentioned by Goudbeek et al. for the Smart Home case [11], there has to be followed a routine for proper analysis of the digital pieces of evidence. Every investigation starts with the preparation and analysis of the smart infrastructure, identifying components, preparing necessary hardware and software tools.

Components Identification and Attribution. A person, who deals with the Smart Application setup, needs to clearly identify used components, sensors, actuators, connectivity and possible information flow and anticipated logic of the system. The picture of the aforementioned setup is shown in the Fig. 4. In this case, all the devices have labels and distinct logos, making them easy to identify and reveal capabilities and technical characteristics.

Fig. 4. Photo of our experimental setup

Live Device On-Chip Access via $JTAG^4/ISP^5/TTL^6$. The next step is to assess whether data can be retrieved when the devices are connected and in *live* mode. It is of crucial importance to follow the *Order of Volatility* as defined by Hegarty et al. [13] to ensure the preservation of all digital data that might be stored either in the permanent memory like flash/SD card or in memory, while will be available only when the device is powered one. Since Arduino has serial communication available, it is possible to connect to the terminal and observe actual communication that is shown in the Fig. 5. From this, it is understandable that MCU is trying to establish MQTT communication and receives data from another component, also successfully identifying some given input pattern. Further, Raspberry Pi board has UART communication, which can be accessed through USB to TTL adapter by connecting TX/RX/GND pins to board pins 6,8 and 10 respectively. Access SoC via UART is given via Linux terminal: *sudo chmod 666 /dev/ttyUSB1; screen /dev/ttyUSB1 115200*

---

[4] Joint Test Action Group standard.
[5] In System Programmer.
[6] Universal Asynchronous Receiver/Transmitter serial convertor.

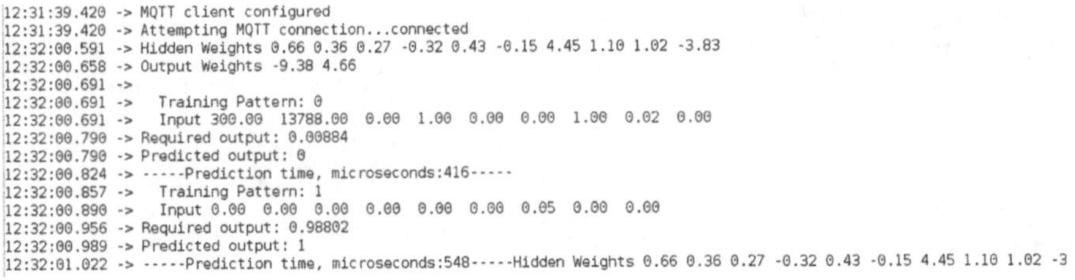
12:31:39.420 -> MQTT client configured
12:31:39.420 -> Attempting MQTT connection...connected
12:32:00.591 -> Hidden Weights 0.66 0.36 0.27 -0.32 0.43 -0.15 4.45 1.10 1.02 -3.83
12:32:00.658 -> Output Weights -9.38 4.66
12:32:00.691 ->
12:32:00.691 -> Training Pattern: 0
12:32:00.691 -> Input 300.00 13788.00 0.00 1.00 0.00 0.00 1.00 0.02 0.00
12:32:00.790 -> Required output: 0.00884
12:32:00.790 -> Predicted output: 0
12:32:00.824 -> -----Prediction time, microseconds:416-----
12:32:00.857 -> Training Pattern: 1
12:32:00.890 -> Input 0.00 0.00 0.00 0.00 0.00 0.00 0.05 0.00 0.00
12:32:00.956 -> Required output: 0.98802
12:32:00.989 -> Predicted output: 1
12:32:01.022 -> -----Prediction time, microseconds:548-----Hidden Weights 0.66 0.36 0.27 -0.32 0.43 -0.15 4.45 1.10 1.02 -3

Fig. 5. Serial monitor from Arduino IDE showing output of live MCU

This process requires an understanding of what kind of boards and technologies are used. Therefore, there can be accessed documentation and discussion forums for each particular component. In our case, by using standard password/login it was possible to log in to the system and check OS information as shown in the Fig. 6.

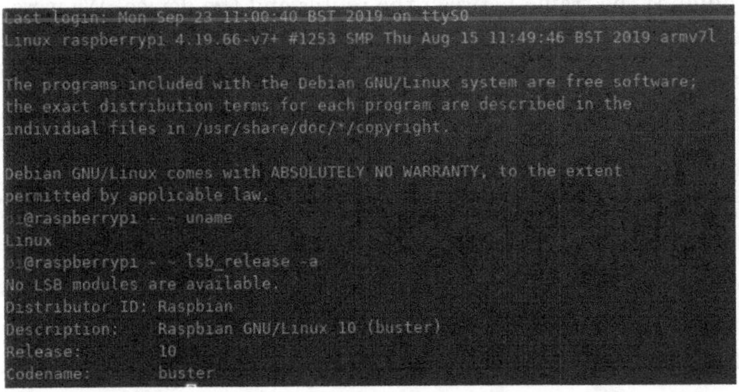
Last login: Mon Sep 23 11:00:40 BST 2019 on ttyS0
Linux raspberrypi 4.19.66-v7+ #1253 SMP Thu Aug 15 11:49:46 BST 2019 armv7l
The programs included with the Debian GNU/Linux system are free software;
the exact distribution terms for each program are described in the
individual files in /usr/share/doc/*/copyright.
Debian GNU/Linux comes with ABSOLUTELY NO WARRANTY, to the extent
permitted by applicable law.
@raspberrypi ~ uname
Linux
@raspberrypi ~ lsb_release -a
No LSB modules are available.
Distributor ID: Raspbian
Description: Raspbian GNU/Linux 10 (buster)
Release: 10
Codename: buster

Fig. 6. UART communication with SoC displaying access terminal and OS information

Live Acquisition of the Network Traffic. Finally, one of the important sources for digital evidential data is network communication within the given IoT infrastructure. To acquire necessary data and technical details, we used Address Resolution Protocol (ARP) Spoofing approach with a help of EtterCAP[7] tool that allows sniffing of a stitched network. The result of the program execution is shown in the Fig. 7.

From EtterCAP we note two important issues: there are two devices with IP addressed *192.168.0.100, 192.168.0.200* that have regular MQTT communication transferring weights (parameters) of the ANN.

Stand-Alone IoT Device Without ML. We use a TTL-to-USB adapter to connect to the UART interface as shown in the Fig. 8. Using the "screen" command we

[7] https://www.sans.org/reading-room/whitepapers/tools/ettercap-primer-1406.

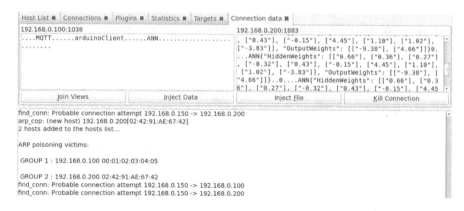

Fig. 7. EtterCAP: intercepted communication between IoT node and IoT gateway

were able to observe sensor output, including timestamps. We connected a laptop to the wifi network. We used ettercap ARP poisoning to capture and record (using tcpdump) the traffic between the router and the device. We were able to capture encrypted UDP-packets between the device and a remote server. Using esptool [2] we were able to read the flash memory over the UART interface. Esptool will inject code into the device to achieve this and reboot the device before and after each operation. It is therefore important to respect the order of volatility. Esptool can also read the virtual memory of the device, but will overwrite some of it in the process.

```
$ screen /dev/ttyUSB0 115200
$ esptool -p /dev/ttyUSB0 dump_mem 0x3ff8_0000 0x142000 esp32_mem1.hex
$ esptool -p /dev/ttyUSB0 dump_mem 0x5000_0000 0x2000 esp32_mem2.hex
$ esptool -p /dev/ttyUSB0 read_flash 0 0x1000000 esp32_flash.hex
$ espefuse -p /dev/ttyUSB0 summary > esp32_efuses.txt
```

Listing 1.1. Retrieving dump of the flash memory from ESP32-WROOM-32D using *esptool*

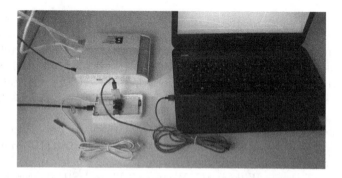

Fig. 8. Extracting data from stand-alone IoT device without ML component

4.2   Lab Work and Analysis

Once *field* work has been finished, the DF process continues with the retrieving and analysis of digital data on each device separately.

IoT Node Artifacts. MCU is, often, custom-made hardware components with proprietary software that will certainly delay the analysis phase. However, there exist common approaches to dump the chip firmware and analyse available data. In our setup, we utilize Avrdude[8] tool with Arduino as AVR in-system programming technique (ISP) to retrieve the data to dump the content of the memory on Arduino Uno as suggested by *Arduino Forensics* [1].

```
$ avrdude −P /dev/ttyUSB0 −F −v −v −c arduino −pm328 −D −Uflash:r:
  ↪ arduino_dump.hex:r
```

Listing 1.2. Retrieving dump of the flash memory from Arduino Uno using *avrdude*

```
$ md5sum: 219de396b61bd3feefc064295fa53828   arduino_dump.hex
$ ls −la: −rw−rw−r— 1   32652 nov.   21 12:17 arduino_dump.hex
```

Listing 1.3. Characteristics of retrieved Arduino flash dump file

The *avrdude* software gives an overview of available memory sections (including flash, EEPROM, fuses, etc) and corresponding hardware device signatures as shown in the Fig. 9.

Memory Type	Mode	Block Poll Delay	Size	Indx	Paged	Page Size	Size	#Pages	MinW	MaxW	Polled ReadBack
eeprom	65	20	4	0	no	1024	4	0	3600	3600	0xff 0xff
flash	65	6	128	0	yes	32768	128	256	4500	4500	0xff 0xff
lfuse	0	0	0	0	no	1	0	0	4500	4500	0x00 0x00
hfuse	0	0	0	0	no	1	0	0	4500	4500	0x00 0x00
efuse	0	0	0	0	no	1	0	0	4500	4500	0x00 0x00
lock	0	0	0	0	no	1	0	0	4500	4500	0x00 0x00
calibration	0	0	0	0	no	1	0	0	0	0	0x00 0x00
signature	0	0	0	0	no	3	0	0	0	0	0x00 0x00

```
Programmer Type : Arduino
Description     : Arduino
Hardware Version: 2
Firmware Version: 1.16
Vtarget         : 0.0 V
Varef           : 0.0 V
Oscillator      : off
SCK period      : 0.1 us

avrdude: AVR device initialized and ready to accept instructions

Reading | ################################################## | 100% 0.00s

avrdude: Device signature = 0x1e950f (probably m328p)
avrdude: Expected signature for ATmega328 is 1E 95 14
```

Fig. 9. Output of the *Avrdude* software verbose output

---

[8] https://www.nongnu.org/avrdude/.

Once the data has been dumped, we use GHex to analyse the content. The first thing that comes to our attention - hard-coded comments about MQTT and IP address as shown in the Fig. 10. Despite the fact that we are not able to retrieve any kind of log files or timestamps, available data can give a clear picture of the device's functionality. Further reverse-engineering and analysis of code will help the investigation, however, takes much more time.

```
0000664600 00 00 29 16 AF 18 16 01 95 16 58 19 0C 16 A1 16 35 17 3F 16 58 17 C3 16 EF   ...).......X.....5.7.[....
0000666019 B5 1B 62 19 19 19 01 E6 15 D6 15 FF FF FF FF FF FF 22 22 5C 5C 62 08 66      ...b..............""\\b.f
0000667A0C 6E 0A 72 0D 74 09 00 48 69 64 64 65 6E 57 65 69 67 68 74 73 00 4F 75 74 70   .n.r.t..HiddenWeights.Outp
0000669475 74 57 65 69 67 68 74 73 00 48 69 64 64 65 6E 20 57 65 69 67 68 74 73 20 00   utWeights.Hidden Weights .
000066AE4F 75 74 70 75 74 20 57 65 69 67 68 74 73 20 00 0D 0A 00 6E 61 6E 00 69 6E 66   Output Weights ....nan.inf
000066C800 6F 76 66 00 31 39 32 2E 31 36 38 2E 30 2E 32 30 30 00 61 72 64 75 69 6E 6F   .ovf.192.168.0.200.arduino
000066E243 6C 69 65 6E 74 00 41 4E 4E 00 20 20 54 72 61 69 6E 69 6E 67 20 50 61 74 74   Client.ANN. Training Patt
000066FC65 72 6E 3A 20 00 20 20 49 6E 70 75 74 20 00 20 20 00 2D 2D 2D 2D 2D 50 72 65   ern: . Input . .-----Pre
0000671664 69 63 74 69 6F 6F 6E 20 74 69 6D 65 2C 20 6D 69 63 72 6F 73 65 63 6F 6E 64 73   diction time, microseconds
000067303A 00 2D 2D 2D 2D 2D 00 FF FF FF FF FF FF FF FF FF FF FF FF FF FF FF FF FF FF   :.-----..................
```

Fig. 10. GHex editor used to analyse flash dump from MCU

IoT Hub/gateway Artifacts. Since Raspberry Pi has Debian installed, that we can refer to general guidelines for *Linux Forensics*, which has broader number of tools and approaches available then Arduino [21,29]. To acquire read-only image copy of the microSD card, we performed following basic operations:

```
$ fdisk −l
Disk /dev/mmcblk0: 14,9 GiB, 15931539456 bytes, 31116288 sectors
Units: sectors of 1 * 512 = 512 bytes
Sector size (logical/physical): 512 bytes / 512 bytes
I/O size (minimum/optimal): 512 bytes / 512 bytes
Disklabel type: dos
Disk identifier: 0x41503d89

Device          Boot   Start       End   Sectors   Size  Id  Type
/dev/mmcblk0p1          8192    532480    524289   256M   c  W95 FAT32 (LBA)
/dev/mmcblk0p2        540672  31116287  30575616  14,6G  83  Linux

$ sudo umount /dev/mmcblk0
$ sudo dd if=/dev/mmcblk0 of=~/sd−card−copy.img
31116288+0 oppfoeringer inn
31116288+0 oppfoeringer ut
15931539456 byte (16 GB), 15 GiB kopiert, 247,108 s, 64,5 MB/s
$ md5sum sd−card−copy.img
93aef0ff0432a512e498153576221ccf  sd−card−copy.img
```

Listing 1.4. Retrieving dump of the microSD card dump from Raspberri PI

Once a read-only copy of the memory card, the following step includes analysis with a widely used software SleuthKit & Autopsy.[9] An example of the folder content, various dates and deleted files are shown in the Fig. 11. The content of the folder may be indicated what kind of software is used, programming languages (C++ in this case) and many other relevant artefacts. Moreover, used dataset (NSL-KDD Cup 99) is also present in the folder, indicating a relation to the network data analysis too. The only executable that is in the folder is *a.out* that requires an additional round of analysis, reverse-engineering, per se.

---

[9] https://www.sleuthkit.org/.

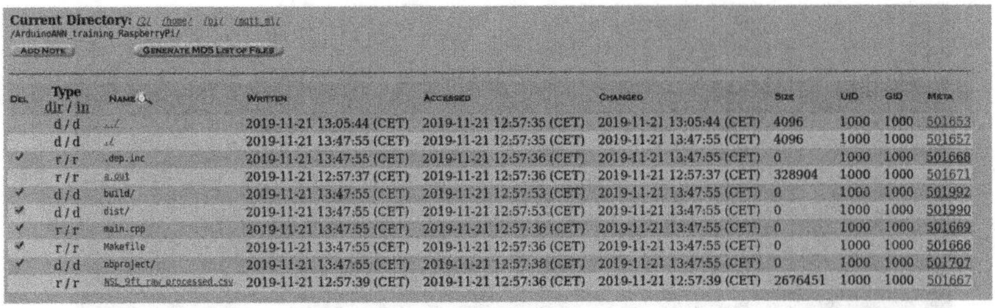

Current Directory: /2/ /home/ /pi/ /mqtt_ml/ /ArduinoANN_training_RaspberryPi/

Add Note | Generate MD5 List of Files

Del.	Type dir / in	Name	Written	Accessed	Changed	Size	UID	GID	Meta
	d / d	../	2019-11-21 13:05:44 (CET)	2019-11-21 12:57:35 (CET)	2019-11-21 13:05:44 (CET)	4096	1000	1000	501653
	d / d	./	2019-11-21 13:47:55 (CET)	2019-11-21 12:57:35 (CET)	2019-11-21 13:47:55 (CET)	4096	1000	1000	501657
✓	r / r	.dep.inc	2019-11-21 13:47:55 (CET)	2019-11-21 12:57:36 (CET)	2019-11-21 13:47:55 (CET)	0	1000	1000	501668
	r / r	a.out	2019-11-21 12:57:37 (CET)	2019-11-21 12:57:36 (CET)	2019-11-21 12:57:37 (CET)	328904	1000	1000	501671
✓	d / d	build/	2019-11-21 13:47:55 (CET)	2019-11-21 12:57:53 (CET)	2019-11-21 13:47:55 (CET)	0	1000	1000	501992
✓	d / d	dist/	2019-11-21 13:47:55 (CET)	2019-11-21 12:57:53 (CET)	2019-11-21 13:47:55 (CET)	0	1000	1000	501990
✓	r / r	main.cpp	2019-11-21 13:47:55 (CET)	2019-11-21 12:57:36 (CET)	2019-11-21 13:47:55 (CET)	0	1000	1000	501669
✓	r / r	Makefile	2019-11-21 13:47:55 (CET)	2019-11-21 12:57:36 (CET)	2019-11-21 13:47:55 (CET)	0	1000	1000	501666
✓	d / d	nbproject/	2019-11-21 13:47:55 (CET)	2019-11-21 12:57:38 (CET)	2019-11-21 13:47:55 (CET)	0	1000	1000	501707
	r / r	NSL_9ft_raw_processed.csv	2019-11-21 12:57:39 (CET)	2019-11-21 12:57:36 (CET)	2019-11-21 12:57:39 (CET)	2676451	1000	1000	501667

Fig. 11. SleuthKit report from imported IoT gateway microSD card image

Machine Learning Component Analysis. Once the software component allegedly attributed to ML is located, the forensics analyst has two challenges: *reverse-engineer any binaries* and *discover application's functionality relevant for the crime investigation.* As mentioned before, any ML application program use *data* to train a specific *model* use for further decision making in Smart Applications. The report is extracted using SleuthKit and shown in the Listing 1.5.

```
$ file /2/home/pi/mqtt_ml/ArduinoANN_training_RaspberryPi/a.out
File Type: ELF 32-bit LSB shared object, ARM, EABI5 version 1 (GNU/Linux
    ↪ ), dynamically linked, interpreter /lib/ld-, for GNU/Linux 3.2.0,
    ↪   BuildID[sha1]=d70d380be66d6e2b6544802dd745707db2834430, not
    ↪ stripped
```

Listing 1.5. Retrieving dump of the microSD card dump from Raspberri PI

The easiest way to understand the functionality of a piece of software is to analyze the source code, which will most likely contain readable variables and function names and self-explainable comments. However, in most cases, the forensics investigators are left only with a compiled binary file. To understand the functionality we can either use commercial IDA Pro or free cross-platform tool Radare2, *Portable reverse-engineering framework*[10] as depicted in Listing 1.6.

```
$ radare2 -aarm ./a.out
> aaa
> s main
> VVV
```

Listing 1.6. Reserse engineering of the *a.out* file

Found artefacts can be linked to the content of the MQTT communication in JSON format that was intercepted earlier using EtterCAP software. Moreover, building function calls graphs, we can get an overview of what kind of operations are performed. Disassembling of ANN training functional routine is shown in the Fig. 12 with the variables names consistent with earlier found digital data.

IoT Device Without ML - Artifacts. The memory and flash were analyzed using GHex. Sensor data was visible in plain text (JSON) and included timestamps. The firmware image can be extracted and analyzed using radare2. The

[10] https://rada.re/n/.

Fig. 12. ARM call function graph disassembly of the binary using Radare2

ESP32 uses a specialized firmware image format, which complicates the reverse-engineering process. Wireshark was used to analyze recorded network packets.

Without an edge device there are fewer available artifacts, and every artifact had its own challenges in terms of extraction, preservation and analysis. The device uses Wifi and the traffic could be captured, but the packets were encrypted and the data is stored in a proprietary cloud. The device had an easily accessible UART interface, but a bootloader must be uploaded to extract artifacts, damaging some artifacts in the process. Esptool is open source, but is platform-specific. It also lacks the functionality of converting firmware images to a standardized format, like ELF32. The flash was not encrypted, but requires reverse-engineering to fully interpret. Furthermore, due to the limited space the data only remains on the device for a limited time before being overwritten by newer data.

5   Digital Forensics Readiness and Cyber-Physical Incident Preparedness

Digital Forensics Readiness is defined as a certain level of readiness of an organization to preserve, collect and analyze any digital data citekarie2017digital. Such data are treated as digital pieces of evidence in any legal or court-related matter. In majority cases, this issue is related to the fact that data have to be stored in an appropriate way. This paper provides an example of a roadmap that can be used when analyzing digital pieces of evidence across any Smart Applications with IoT-based distributed infrastructure. Data retention policies are established in the organization to follow a common practice of preservation data that further can be used to speed up any involved forensics investigations or incident response. Since IoT-bases systems have naturally distributed versatile resources, one needs to ensure *pre-investigation readiness* and *real-time integration* as a key to successful digital forensics investigation in IoT in future [31].

The *core difference* of Smart Applications from other IoT applications is the existence of the ML processing mechanism, which implies that the decisions made by separate components based on the data might not be straight-forward. From the previous section, we can reconstruct the following scenario. The data are being processed on IoT gateways using the ML model called ANN. Further, the trained model (weights of the neuron connections) is being transmitted via Ethernet connection to IoT nodes with the help of the MQTT protocol. The protocol was not encrypted, so we used the ARP spoofing attack to intercept traffic between those two components. IoT node has open serial communication that gives a hint about ML model usage, which is also confirmed by analysis of string comments in dumped flash memory with the help of Arduino Forensics. Moreover, IoT gateway has Debian OS leaving many opportunities for Linux Forensics, such as file system analysis. After a closer look at the content of the folders, a network intrusion data set was found along with the binary file compiled for ARM. Reverse-engineering and disassembly of the binary file will reveal internal logic and functions used for ANN training. While understanding of hardware and software technologies is a crucial part of any modern investigation, there is also a need for cross-disciplinary awareness and expertise exchange to ensure a correct understanding of Smart Applications. Subsequently, it reflects aspects of their possible involvement in any criminal activities. Our belief is that technology awareness and expert knowledge will help to move from *Reactive* Digital Crime Investigation to *Proactive* Crime Prevention and Incident Response when it comes to any illegal activities in Smart Applications.

6   Conclusions and Discussions

This paper presents the thorny path of the Digital Forensics expert handling Smart Devices and Smart Applications. It is clear that the traditional understanding of Computer Forensics is under constant evolvement. Static data and well-known technologies are no longer a State of the Art. With the advancement of Smart Devices, IoT and later Smart Applications, a forensics expert is facing Big Data paradigm, proprietary software, previously unseen hardware components and Cloud Computing involvement. However, the growing demand for intelligent data analytics brings Machine Learning models in every component of the IoT ecosystem. Despite the complexity of such data analytics, one will need to utilize insights into how the data are processed and what kind of decisions are made. This will ensure timely response to incidents and proactive crime prevention in modern societies living in Smart Cities. This paper presented an example of a Digital Forensics Investigation roadmap in a Smart Application, explaining a whole range of forensics activities needed for a clearer understanding of the key value of any investigation - data, or digital pieces of evidence.

Even in an ecosystem without edge-devices and machine learning, the process is similar and has similar challenges. Especially the lack of standardization – every IoT platform (and cloud platform) requires specialized tools and knowledge to reverse-engineer the hardware and software. We expect cooperation between the forensic investigator and various actors, including the manufacturer, the developer and the cloud provider, to become a crucial part of forensic investigation.

Acknowledgement. Authors would like to thank to the Department of Information Security and Communication Technology (IIK) at the Norwegian University of Science and Technology for support and funding of this contribution. Moreover, this research has received funding from the Swedish Civil Contingencies Agency (MSB) through the research center Resilient Information and Control Systems (RICS).

References

1. The application of reverse engineering techniques against the Arduino microcontroller to acquire uploaded applications (2014). Accessed 19 Nov 2019
2. Ahlberg, F.: esptool (2020). https://github.com/espressif/esptool. Accessed 29 May 2020
3. Alenezi, A., Atlam, H., Alsagri, R., Alassafi, M., Wills, G.: IoT forensics: a state-of-the-art review, challenges and future directions. In: Proceedings of the 4th International Conference on Complexity, Future Information Systems and Risk (2019)
4. Antonakakis, M., et al.: Understanding the Mirai botnet. In: 26th USENIX Security Symposium, pp. 1093–1110 (2017)
5. Damshenas, M., Dehghantanha, A., Mahmoud, R., bin Shamsuddin, S.: Forensics investigation challenges in cloud computing environments. In: Proceedings Title: 2012 International Conference on Cyber Security, Cyber Warfare and Digital Forensic (CyberSec), pp. 190–194. IEEE (2012)
6. Delicato, F.C., Pires, P.F., Batista, T., Cavalcante, E., Costa, B., Barros, T.: Towards an IoT ecosystem. In: Proceedings of the First International Workshop on Software Engineering for Systems-of-Systems, pp. 25–28. ACM (2013)
7. Dengler, S., Awad, A., Dressler, F.: Sensor/actuator networks in smart homes for supporting elderly and handicapped people. In: 21st International Conference on Advanced Information Networking and Applications Workshops (AINAW 2007), vol. 2, pp. 863–868. IEEE (2007)
8. Ericsson: Internet of things forecast (2019). https://www.ericsson.com/en/mobility-report/internet-of-things-forecast. Accessed 04 Oct 2019
9. Esposito, C., Castiglione, A., Pop, F., Choo, K.K.R.: Challenges of connecting edge and cloud computing: a security and forensic perspective. IEEE Cloud Comput. **4**(2), 13–17 (2017)
10. Espressif: Esp32-wroom-32d (2019). https://www.espressif.com/sites/default/files/documentation/esp32-wroom-32d_esp32-wroom-32u_datasheet_en.pdf. Accessed 29 May 2020
11. Goudbeek, A., Choo, K.K.R., Le-Khac, N.A.: A forensic investigation framework for smart home environment. In: 2018 17th IEEE International Conference on Trust, Security and Privacy in Computing and Communications/12th IEEE International Conference on Big Data Science and Engineering (TrustCom/BigDataSE), pp. 1446–1451. IEEE (2018)
12. Grance, T., Chevalier, S., Scarfone, K.K., Dang, H.: Guide to integrating forensic techniques into incident response. Technical report (2006)
13. Hegarty, R., Lamb, D.J., Attwood, A.: Digital evidence challenges in the internet of things. In: INC, pp. 163–172 (2014)
14. Koen, R., Olivier, M.S.: The use of file timestamps in digital forensics. In: ISSA, pp. 1–16. Citeseer (2008)
15. Kolias, C., Kambourakis, G., Stavrou, A., Voas, J.: DDoS in the IoT: Mirai and other botnets. Computer **50**(7), 80–84 (2017)

16. Kononenko, I., Kukar, M.: Machine Learning and Data Mining: Introduction to Principles and Algorithms. Horwood Publishing Limited (2007)
17. Lillis, D., Becker, B., O'Sullivan, T., Scanlon, M.: Current challenges and future research areas for digital forensic investigation. arXiv (2016)
18. Oriwoh, E., Jazani, D., Epiphaniou, G., Sant, P.: Internet of things forensics: challenges and approaches. In: 9th IEEE International Conference on Collaborative Computing: Networking, Applications and Worksharing, pp. 608–615. IEEE (2013)
19. Perumal, S., Norwawi, N.M., Raman, V.: Internet of things (IoT) digital forensic investigation model: top-down forensic approach methodology. In: 2015 Fifth International Conference on Digital Information Processing and Communications (ICDIPC), pp. 19–23. IEEE (2015)
20. Pollitt, M.: A history of digital forensics. In: Chow, K.-P., Shenoi, S. (eds.) DigitalForensics 2010. IFIP AICT, vol. 337, pp. 3–15. Springer, Heidelberg (2010). https://doi.org/10.1007/978-3-642-15506-2_1
21. Pomeranz, H.: Linux forensics (for non-linux folks). http://www.deer-run.com/~hal/LinuxForensicsForNon-LinuxFolks.pdf. Accessed 21 Nov 2019
22. Postscapes: IoT standards and protocols (2019). https://www.postscapes.com/internet-of-things-protocols/. Accessed 04 Oct 2019
23. Sadeghi, A., Wachsmann, C., Waidner, M.: Security and privacy challenges in industrial internet of things. In: 2015 52nd ACM/EDAC/IEEE Design Automation Conference (DAC), pp. 1–6, June 2015
24. Satyanarayanan, M.: The emergence of edge computing. Computer **50**(1), 30–39 (2017)
25. Schatsky, D., Kumar, N., Bumb, S.: Intelligent IoT: Bringing the power of AI to the internet of things (2017)
26. Shalaginov, A.: Soft computing and hybrid intelligence for decision support in forensics science. In: IEEE Intelligence and Security Informatics, pp. 304–309 (2016)
27. Shalaginov, A.: Advancing Neuro-Fuzzy Algorithm for Automated Classification in Largescale Forensic and Cybercrime Investigations: Adaptive Machine Learning for Big Data Forensic. Ph.D. thesis, Norwegian University of Science and Technology (2018)
28. Shalaginov, A., Semeniuta, O., Alazab, M.: MEML: resource-aware MQTT-based machine learning for network attacks detection on IoT edge devices. In: Proceedings of the 12th IEEE/ACM International Conference on Utility and Cloud Computing Companion, pp. 123–128. ACM (2019)
29. Willis, C.: Forensics with linux 101 or how to do forensics for free (2003). https://www.blackhat.com/presentations/bh-usa-03/bh-us-03-willis-c/bh-us-03-willis.pdf. Accessed 21 Nov 2019
30. Yusoff, Y., Ismail, R., Hassan, Z.: Common phases of computer forensics investigation models. Int. J. Comput. Sci. Inf. Technol. **3**(3), 17–31 (2011)
31. Zulkipli, N.H.N., Alenezi, A., Wills, G.B.: IoT forensic: bridging the challenges in digital forensic and the internet of things. In: International Conference on Internet of Things, Big Data and Security, vol. 2, pp. 315–324. SCITEPRESS (2017)

A Microservice-Based Industrial Control System Architecture Using Cloud and MEC

Yu Kaneko$^{(\boxtimes)}$, Yuhei Yokoyama, Nobuyuki Monma, Yoshiki Terashima, Keiichi Teramoto, Takuya Kishimoto, and Takeshi Saito

Corporate Research and Development Center, Toshiba Corporation, Kawasaki, Japan
yu1.kaneko@toshiba.co.jp

Abstract. Cloud computing has been adapted for various application areas. Several research projects are underway to migrate Industrial Control Systems (ICSs) to the public cloud. Some functions of ICSs require real-time processing that is difficult to migrate to the public cloud because network latency of the internet is unpredictable. Fog computing is a new computing paradigm that could address this latency issue. In particular, Multi-access Edge Computing (MEC) is a fog computing environment integrated with the 5G network, and therefore the real-time processing requirement of ICSs could be satisfied by using MEC. In this paper, we propose a microservice-based ICS architecture using the cloud and fog computing. In the architecture, each function of an ICS is implemented as a microservice and its execution locations are determined by an algorithm minimizing the total usage fee for cloud and fog computing while satisfying the real-time processing requirement. The proposed architecture and placement algorithm are evaluated by simulation under the scenario of a virtual power plant that manages distributed energy resources. The simulation result shows the proposed placement algorithm suppresses VM usage fee while satisfying the requirement of a real-time control function.

Keywords: Industrial Control System · Cloud · Fog · 5G · MEC

1 Introduction

Cloud computing has been adapted for various application areas. Users of cloud computing are interested in fast deployment, scalability, and reducing the cost of applications. In view of those advantages of cloud computing, several research projects are underway to migrate Industrial Control Systems (ICSs) to the public cloud [21]. Some functions of ICSs require real-time processing, for example, controlling industrial devices such as robot arms in a factory or storage batteries in a power plant. It is difficult for cloud-based ICSs to control industrial devices in real-time because the internet, a large network whose latency is unpredictable, exists between the public cloud and the industrial devices.

© Springer Nature Switzerland AG 2020
A. Katangur et al. (Eds.): EDGE 2020, LNCS 12407, pp. 18–32, 2020.
https://doi.org/10.1007/978-3-030-59824-2_2

Fog computing is a new computing paradigm whose computing resources tend to be less than in the case of cloud computing, but deployed closer to data sources, including industrial devices [4]. Thus, fog computing could provide low and predictable network latency for applications. One of the examples of fog computing is Multi-access Edge Computing (MEC) defined by ETSI [1]. MEC infrastructure is highly integrated with telecommunication providers' datacenters at the edge of the 5G network. ICSs running on MEC can utilize the ultra low-latency 5G network to realize real-time control and can analyze the status of industrial devices quickly. On the other hand, the usage fee for MEC is higher than that for the public cloud because: 1) MEC has limited computing resources, and thus economies of scale do not work well, unlike in the case of the public cloud that has hyper scale computing resources, and 2) MEC can provide not only cloud computing capability but also additional functionality such as low-latency and wideband communication. To suppress the operation cost of an ICS, it is important to execute only real-time functions by fog computing whereas non-real-time functions should be executed in the cloud. It means that the functions of an ICS are distributed across the cloud and fog computing environments. A microservice approach is suitable for such situation. If each function were implemented as a microservice with container technology such as Docker[1], it could be executed in the cloud or fog without any modification and could interact with other functions via APIs.

ICSs have many functions, and thus an ICS is composed of a large number of microservices. Efficient management of a large number of microservices is a typical issue in the operation of microservice-based systems. Thus, a service placement algorithm that determines the locations of services while properly considering the operation cost and requirements of real-time processing is necessary from the perspective of ICS operators. Conventional placement algorithms minimize processing latency, or network traffic or battery consumption, and so on. To the best of our knowledge, the literature includes no study on service placement algorithms that considers both real-time processing and the usage fees for cloud and fog computing.

In this paper, a microservice-based ICS architecture utilizing the cloud and MEC properly and a service placement algorithm are proposed. It is supposed that the proposed algorithm will be used by ICS operators, and therefore we focus on minimizing the usage fees for cloud and fog while keeping deadlines of real-time processing. A Virtual Power Plant (VPP) system that manages Distributed Energy Resources (DERs) is considered as an example of an ICS.

The rest of the paper is organized as follows. Section 2 explains background knowledge concerning the cloud, fog computing, ICSs, and VPP. The proposed microservice-based ICS architecture and service placement algorithm are described in Sect. 3. Section 4 explains a simulator for evaluation of the proposed algorithm. The proposed algorithm is evaluated in Sect. 5. Section 6 summarizes related works. Finally, we conclude our proposal in Sect. 7.

---

[1] https://www.docker.com/.

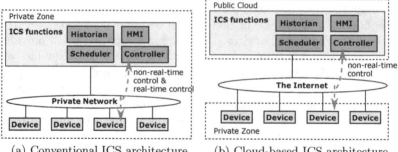

(a) Conventional ICS architecture   (b) Cloud-based ICS architecture

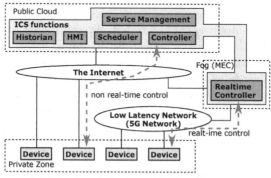

(c) Cloud and fog based ICS architecture

Fig. 1. Three types of ICS architecture. Historian is a time-series database storing the status of industrial devices. Human Machine Interface (HMI) is a function that visualizes the device status for operators. Scheduler schedules the start time of operations including a controller function.

2 Background

2.1 Cloud and Fog Computing

Cloud computing is an environment where users can build, deploy, and run any applications without buying hardware assets [2]. It provides various services for users, such as Virtual Machine (VM) services, container services, and storage services. As in the case of utilities such as water, gas, and electricity, users pay only for the resources they consume. Amazon Web Services (AWS)[2], Microsoft Azure[3], Google Cloud[4] are examples of public cloud. Various kinds of systems have migrated from on-premises to the cloud because of the cloud's advantages such as flexibility, inexpensiveness, and scalability.

---

[2] https://aws.amazon.com/.

[3] https://azure.microsoft.com/.

[4] https://cloud.google.com/.

Fog computing is a computing environment deployed closer to data sources. It can provide not only capabilities similar to those of the cloud, but also low network latency for data sources for applications. MEC is a fog computing environment defined by ETSI [1]. It is highly integrated with telecommunication providers' datacenters at the edge of the 5G network. Applications running on MEC can utilize the ultra low-latency 5G network and interact with devices located in a certain area via the 5G communication channel. AWS Wavelength[5] is an example of MEC that provides users with AWS services such as AWS EC2[6].

MEC has limited computing resources compared to those of the cloud. Therefore, the usage fee for MEC is assumed to be higher than that for the cloud because, unlike in the case of the public cloud, economies of scale do not work well [1]. Another reason is that MEC can provide not only cloud computing capability but also additional functionality such as ultra low-latency and ultra-wideband communication. From the perspective of application operators, using cloud and fog properly according to the requirements of an application is important for suppressing the cost of operation.

2.2   Industrial Control Systems

Industrial Control Systems (ICSs) are systems that manage various industrial devices. One example of an ICS is a factory automation system that monitors and controls conveyor belts, robot arms, and so on, to manufacture products in a factory. Another example is a building automation system that monitors and controls air-conditioning systems, room lights, and so on, to improve the comfort and energy efficiency of a building.

High availability, stability, and real-time operations are required for ICSs. To achieve these requirements, ICSs have been constructed with special hardware and deployed close to industrial devices because some devices should be controlled in real-time. The real-time control is performed via a private network as shown in Fig. 1a. The special hardware tends to be expensive because of its redundant architecture that is intended to achieve high availability. Therefore, in order to reduce the construction costs of ICSs, research projects are underway to deploy ICSs in the cloud environment without special hardware [6]. This cloud-based ICS architecutre is depicted in Fig. 1b. However, it is difficult for cloud-based ICSs to perform real-time control because the internet, whose network latency is unpredictable, exists between the cloud and industrial devices. In this paper, we propose an ICS architecture based on cloud and MEC to solve the network latency issue as shown in Fig. 1c.

2.3   Virtual Power Plant

A Virtual Power Plant (VPP) is an ICS that aggregates Distributed Energy Resources (DERs), such as storage batteries, thermal storage tanks, photovoltaic

---

[5] https://aws.amazon.com/wavelength.
[6] https://aws.amazon.com/ec2/.

Table 1. Five energy classes in an energy trading market of Japan (FCR: Frequency Containment Reserve, S-FRR: Synchronized Frequency Restoration Reserve, FCR: Frequency Restoration Reserve, RR: Replacement Reserve)

	FCR	S-FRR	FRR	RR	RR-FIT
Control duration	5 min or over	30 min or over	30 min or over	3 h	3 h
Control interval	-	0.5 s to 1 min	1 min to 10 min	1 min to 10 min	30 min

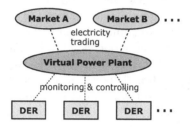

Fig. 2. High level architecture of virtual power plant

power generators, wind power generators, electric vehicles, so as to act as a power plant [13]. VPPs are required to cooperate with energy trading markets and control DERs accurately via a network to adjust power supply and demand. High-level architecture of a typical VPP system is shown in Fig. 2. A VPP monitors and controls DERs with a network protocol such as ECHONET Lite^{TM}(IEC62394) [10] or IEC61850 [11] and an interval of control is decided according to results of transactions in energy trading markets. For example, five energy classes described in Table 1 will be traded in the new energy trading market in Japan[7]. If a VPP trades energy class "RR-FIT" in the market and the transaction is completed, the VPP has to monitor and control some DERs every few minutes. This control process could be performed from the public cloud. On the other hand, if transaction of energy class "S-FFR" is completed, the VPP has to monitor and control every 500 ms. This control is difficult to perform from the public cloud because the total time of 1) network latency of the internet, 2) processing time of the control function on a VM in the cloud, and 3) processing time of the received control signal on a DER is larger than 500 ms. MEC is useful to reduce network latency. Although DERs except for electric vehicles do not move, wireless communication including 5G can reduce the cost of wiring a large number of distributed DERs.

3 Proposed ICS Architecture and Algorithm

In this section, the proposed ICS architecture and the service placement algorithms are described. We assume that operators of ICSs are users of the cloud

---

[7] https://www.meti.go.jp/shingikai/enecho/denryoku_gas/denryoku_gas/seido_kento/pdf/028_05_00.pdf.

and MEC. Operators of an ICS need to pay a usage fee to the cloud or MEC service provider according to the amount of resources consumed by the ICS.

3.1 Microservice-Based ICS Architecture

As shown in Fig. 1c, the proposed ICS architecture is based on the cloud and MEC. Each function of an ICS is implemented as a microservice and deployed on a container platform. Considering information such as usage fees for cloud and fog, required computing and network resources, the requirement for real-time processing, the service management decides locations of functions (services). Basically, non-real-time functions such as historian, HMI, and scheduler are located in the cloud and real-time functions such as real-time control are handled by MEC. Functions handled by MEC can access industrial devices through the low-latency 5G network.

Multiple cloud and MEC can be used together for construction of an ICS. For example, an ICS can be constructed based on AWS EC2 and Microsoft Azure. Because ICS functions are implemented as microservices, these functions can be deployed in various environments that have container capability.

The proposed architecture can enjoy the advantages of both cloud and fog computing, and therefore it is flexible, inexpensive, and scalable, and could perform real-time processing.

3.2 VPP System Based on the Proposed Architecture

There are several ICSs that could be applicable to the proposed architecture [22]. In this paper, we apply the proposed architecture to a VPP system (Fig. 3). The following microservices are the minimum set of functions of a VPP.

- Asset management service: It manages characteristics and statistics of DERs such as adjustable power and response time to control signal.
- Demand forecast service: It forecasts energy demand to build trading strategies.
- Trading service: It trades capability of power adjustment via energy markets considering DER statistics and result of demand forecast. An example of energy classes traded is shown in Table 1.
- Control service: It monitors and controls a DER according to the transaction result. It is deployed for each DER during control duration.
- Service management service: It decides suitable placement of control services. It also deploys VMs on the cloud or fog and runs control services.

Typical process sequence of the VPP system is described below.

1. The trading service trades via energy markets considering DER information.
2. If a transaction was completed, control datetime, duration, control interval, and target DERs are fixed. The trading service sends that information to the management service.

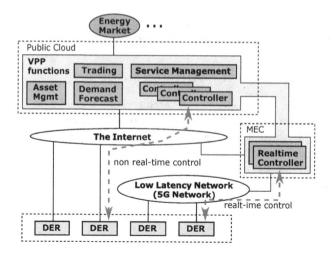

Fig. 3. VPP system based on the proposed architecture.

3. The management service determines locations for each control service according to the transaction result by using the placement algorithm described in Subsect. 3.3. The locations should be decided to keep the required control interval and minimize the running cost of control services.
4. The management service boots necessary VMs at the locations determined by the algorithm and runs control services on the VMs.
5. The control services repeat controlling and monitoring of the target DERs during control duration.
6. The management service stops the control services and shuts down VMs that have no active control services.

3.3   Control Service Placement Algorithm

The placement algorithm assumes that cloud and fog computing environments are provided by certain providers and use of their computing resources incurs charges. The management service possesses information on the cloud and fog computing environments, such as usage fee for VMs and network latency for DERs. Processing times of control signals for DERs are also known. The total amount of cloud or fog computing resources is unknown to ICS developers because we assume that ICS developers and cloud or fog providers are different, and therefore the algorithm does not consider the remaining resources. The amount of resources (CPU, memory, storage) required to run the control service are also known in advance by simple evaluation, and thus suitable VM instance types for the control service can be determined. The placement algorithm does not need to consider multiple VM instance types. We do not assume service migration during control duration because it could decrease quality of control.

Algorithm 1 LATENCY

Require:
  R_i = required control interval
  1: **function** SELECT_DCs_BY_LATENCY(R)
  2:     $candidates = \{\}$
  3:     **for** DC in $allDCs$ **do**
  4:         $I_c = DC.latency \times 2 + T_{sp} + T_{dp}$
  5:         **if** $I_c <= R$ **then**
  6:             push DC to $candidates$
  7:         **end if**
  8:     **end for**
  9:     **return** $candidates$
 10: **end function**
 11: $candidates = $ SELECT_DCs_BY_LATENCY(R_i)
 12: $targetDC$ is selected randomly from $candidates$; Run a VM and a control service

---

Three placement algorithms: 1) LATENCY, 2) LATENCY-COST, and 3) LATENCY-COST-VM, are described as follows. Cloud and fog environment are referred to as "datacenter (DC)" in the following description of the algorithms.

LATENCY Algorithm. The LATENCY algorithm considers network latency from DCs to DERs to keep the control interval condition. Network latency can be measured with software such as `ping` command. It calculates estimated control interval I_c for each DC by (1) and selects a DC as a candidate DC only if the estimated control interval I_c is less than or equal to the required control interval.

$$I_c = L_n \times 2 + T_{sp} + T_{dp} \tag{1}$$

L_n, T_{sp}, and T_{dp} denote network latency, processing time of a control service on a VM, and processing time of a DER, respectively. These parameters can be known in advance by simple evaluation as mentioned above. Then, it selects one DC from the candidate DCs randomly. The service management boots a VM on the selected DC and runs a control service on the VM. The pseudo-code is described as Algorithm 1.

LATENCY-COST Algorithm. The LATENCY-COST algorithm considers not only network latency but also usage fee for VMs. First, it selects candidate DCs in the same manner as the LATENCY algorithm. Second, it selects a DC that has the minimum VM usage fee from the candidate DCs. Then, the service management boots a VM on the DC and runs a control service. The pseudo-code is described as Algorithm 2.

Algorithm 2 LATENCY-COST

Require:

    R_i = required control interval

 1: **function** SELECT_DC_BY_FEE(DCs)

 2:    $minUsageFee = 999999999; targetDC = null$

 3:    **for** DC in DCs **do**

 4:        **if** $minUsageFee > DC.usageFee$ **then**

 5:            $targetDC = DC; minUsageFee = DC.usageFee$

 6:        **end if**

 7:    **end for**

 8:    **return** $targetDC$

 9: **end function**

10: $candidates = $ SELECT_DCs_BY_LATENCY(R_i)

11: $targetDC = $ SELECT_DC_BY_FEE($candidates$)

12: Run a VM and a control service in the $targetDC$

LATENCY-COST-VM Algorithm. The LATENCY and LATENCY-COST algorithm always boots a new VM for a control service. The LATENCY-COST-VM algorithm considers running multiple control services on the same VM. First, the algorithm selects a DC in the same manner as the LATENCY-COST algorithm. Next, the algorithm estimates the additional usage fee for running the control service for each running VM. If the minimum estimated usage fee is less than the usage fee for using a new VM, the service management runs the control service on the running VM. Otherwise, the service management boots a VM and runs the control service. A drawback of the algorithm is the increase of processing time of each control service (T_{sp}), which could violate the control interval requirement. The pseudo-code is described as Algorithm 3.

4   Simulator for the Proposed Algorithm

There are several simulators that can simulate cloud and fog computing environments such as iFogSim [8], EdgeCloudSim [20], and PureEdgeSim [12]. We use PureEdgeSim in the evaluation because it can easily configure hundreds of devices and it can define specifications of datacenters, hosts, and VMs.

To evaluate the proposed algorithm, we extend the PureEdgeSim simulator. The control service of the VPP system is modeled as a process that repeats *active* state and *inactive* state at each control interval during the control duration. As shown in Fig. 4, in the active state, the control service calculates a control value and sends it to the DER. The state of the control service is inactive until the start time of the next control interval.

The active state process is implemented as a control task extended `Task` class of PureEdgeSim. Thus, a control service is expressed as a sequence of control tasks. The `TasksGenerator` of PureEdgeSim is extended to create the control task. The extended generator basically creates a control task at the start time of each control interval. However, the generator does not create a control task

---

Algorithm 3 LATENCY-COST-VM

Require:

R_i = required control interval, D = control duration, D_f = finish time of D

1: **function** ESTIMATE_FEE(VM, D_f)
2:    $finishTime = 0$
3:    **for** $service$ in $VM.runningControlServices$ **do**
4:        **if** $service.finishTime > finishTime$ **then**
5:            $finishTime = service.finishTime$
6:        **end if**
7:    **end for**
8:    $additionalRuntime = D_f - finishTime$
9:    **if** $additionalRuntime <= 0$ **then**
10:        **return** 0
11:    **else**
12:        **return** $additionalRuntime \times VM.usageFee$
13:    **end if**
14: **end function**
15: $candidates = $ SELECT_DCs_BY_LATENCY(R_i)
16: $targetDC = $ SELECT_DC_BY_FEE($candidates$)
17: $minUsageFee = targetDC.usageFee \times D$; $targetVM = null$
18: **for** VM in $runningVMs$ of $candidates$ **do**
19:    $estimatedFee = $ ESTIMATE_FEE(VM, D_f)
20:    **if** $estimatedFee < minUsageFee$ **then**
21:        $minUsageFee = estimatedFee$; $targetVM = VM$
22:    **end if**
23: **end for**
24: **if** $targetVM$ is NOT $null$ **then**
25:    Run a control service on the $targetVM$
26: **else**
27:    Run a VM and a control service in the $targetDC$
28: **end if**

---

if the status of a DER has not been returned, because the status of a DER is required to calculate the next control value for the DER. It means that large network latency or large processing time of DER would cause delay in creation of a control task.

Cloud and fog computing environments are implemented as an extended class of `EdgeDataCenter` of PureEdgeSim. It is extended to have properties such as network latency for DERs and usage fee for VMs. In addition, the proposed placement algorithms (Subsect. 3.3) are implemented as an extended orchestrator.

5   Evaluation

5.1   Evaluation Setup

Figure 5 shows the assumed environment in the evaluation. There are two public clouds, cloud1 and cloud2. Cloud1 and MEC1 and the hundred DERs are located

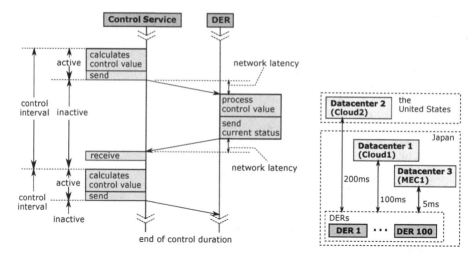

Fig. 4. The model of the control service   **Fig. 5.** Simulation Environment

in the same area of Japan. The other cloud (cloud2) is located in the United States. Most of the VPP functions such as the trading service and the service management run on cloud1. Control services of the VPP can run on cloud1 or cloud2 or MEC1 to control the DERs. Network latency for the DERs is different between cloud1, cloud2, and MEC1. The network latency from cloud1 to the DERs is 100 ms and that from cloud2 is 200 ms. MEC1 is deployed close to the DERs, and thus network latency between MEC1 and the DERs is 5 ms.

Table 2 shows the evaluation parameters. Duration of the simulation is one day and each DER is traded via an energy market once a day. Control services are generated for each DER in the simulation, and therefore the number of control services is the same as the number of DERs. We assume that cloud1, cloud2, and MEC1 have sufficient amounts of resources for running 100 control services. Start times of control services are decided at random. Control duration of all control services is 30 min. There are 4 types of control interval, namely, 0.5 s, 1 s, 5 s, and 60 s, which are equivalent to energy class S-FRR or FRR (Table 1). Control interval type is decided at random for each control service. The task generator creates a control task sequence for each control service. MIPS of a VM is 4000 and MIPS of a control task is 1000, and thus a control task is completed in 250 ms if the VM has only one control task. The VM usage fees for cloud1 and cloud2 are determined according to usage fee for t2.small VM instance in the Tokyo region and the North California region of AWS EC2. The usage fee for MEC is unclear at the time of writing the paper. We assume the usage fee for MEC is 0.1 \$/h, which is larger than the usage fee for cloud.

The three service placement algorithms described in Subsect. 3.3 are evaluated 30 times with the parameters in Table 2. In addition, the following two algorithms are also evaluated 30 times for the purpose of comparison.

Table 2. Evaluation Parameters

Parameter	Value
Evaluation duration (hour)	24
Number of DERs	100
Number of control services	100
Control duration (min)	30
Control interval (sec)	0.5, 1.0, 5.0, 60.0
MIPS of a VM, control task	4000, 1000
CPU core of a VM	1
DER processing time (T_{dp}) (ms)	100
Network latency of MEC1, cloud1, cloud2 (L_n) (ms)	5, 100, 200
VM usage fee of MEC1, cloud1, cloud2 ($/h)	0.1000, 0.0304, 0.0276

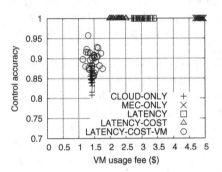

Fig. 6. VM usage fee vs. control accuracy

Fig. 7. Destination of service placement

– CLOUD-ONLY algorithm uses cloud1 or cloud2 for service placement.
– MEC-ONLY algorithm uses only MEC1 for service placement.

Total usage fee for VMs and control accuracy are measured in the evaluation. Control accuracy is calculated by $\frac{N_f}{N}$. N and N_f denote total number of control tasks and number of control tasks completed in the control interval, respectively.

5.2 Evaluation Result

All evaluation results, VM usage fee and control accuracy, are shown in Fig. 6. Average VM usage fee and control accuracy are summarized in Table 3. Service placement ratio of each algorithm are shown in Fig. 7.

The usage fee for CLOUD-ONLY is low and stable as expected because the usage fee for the cloud is low. The usage fee for MEC-ONLY is the highest of all the algorithms and its control accuracy is 1.0, which means all control tasks are completed successfully in the control interval. Control accuracy of LATENCY is

Table 3. Average usage fee and control accuracy of each algorithm

Algorithm	Average usage fee ($/h)	Average accuracy
CLOUD-ONLY	1.4122	0.8564
MEC-ONLY	4.8450	1.0000
LATENCY	3.0150	1.0000
LATENCY-COST	2.2456	1.0000
LATENCY-COST-VM	1.4604	0.8967

also 1.0 and its usage fee is lower than that for MEC-ONLY because some of the control services whose control interval is 1 s or 5 s or 60 s were executed in the cloud1 or cloud2 (Fig. 7). The usage fee for LATENCY-COST is lower than that for LATENCY. In the simulation environment, control services whose control interval is 0.5 s should be placed in MEC1 to keep the interval, whereas control services whose interval is 1 s or 5 s or 60 s can be placed in cloud1 or cloud2 or MEC1. Thus, the LATENCY-COST algorithm does not selects cloud1 because its usage fee is higher than that of cloud2 (Fig. 7).

Of all the algorithms, LATENCY-COST-VM has the lowest usage fee because it places multiple control services on a VM. In other words, LATENCY-COST-VM runs several VMs whereas other algorithms run 100 VMs. However, running multiple services on a VM increases processing time of the control task (T_{sp}), which causes cases in which a control task cannot be finished in the control interval. To avoid this issue and improve control accuracy, the LATENCY-COST-VM algorithm should consider the increase of processing time of a control task. It should place multiple control services on the same VM only if all control tasks will be completed during the control interval. This algorithm improvement is a future work.

6   Related Work

There are research projects that aim to migrate ICSs to the cloud so as to enjoy its flexibility, inexpensiveness, and scalability [9,21]. However, real-time processing is difficult for cloud-based ICSs. To address this issue, an approach in which fog computing is utilized together with cloud is attracting attention. The authors of [22] implement a system based on both cloud and fog in order to control robot arms in a factory. Cloud and fog architecture is also applicable to other ICSs such as building management systems [5] and electrical substations [15]. To operate an ICS based on both cloud and fog effectively, algorithms that determine execution locations for each function of an ICS are important.

There are several research on service placement algorithms. Those algorithms differ in terms of what each algorithm optimizes and what kind of conditions it considers. Considering computing resource and network performance, the algorithms proposed in [16,17] minimize processing time. In [18], a service placement tool is proposed that considers network latency. The authors of [14] implement a platform that decides service placement, considering network traffic and batteries of mobile devices. An algorithm maximizing the number of tasks processed by nodes in cloud or fog is described in [19]. These algorithms [14, 16–19] do not consider the usage fee for cloud or fog or edge.

An algorithm proposed in [3] minimizes the cost of task processing, considering the mobility of user devices. An algorithm proposed in [7] also minimizes the operation cost of medical cyber-physical systems. However, these algorithms [3, 7] do not consider deadline of the processing time.

Our proposed algorithm (Subsect. 3.3) considers the usage fee and the processing time deadline. It minimizes usage fees for cloud and fog while keeping the deadline for real-time processing of ICSs.

7   Conclusion

In this paper, we proposed a microservice-based ICS architecture and the optimal service placement algorithm that decides service placements to minimize the usage fee for ICS functions while satisfying the real-time requirements of the functions. An evaluation considering cloud and fog environments is performed with simulation and the proposed algorithm could decide control service locations to minimize its operation cost and satisfy the real-time requirements.

We intend to perform simulations of more realistic cases, for example, coexistence of multiple applications, using not VMs but a container service such as AWS Fargate[8], considering more DERs. In addition, we intend to implement the proposed architecture and the placement algorithm in a real environment.

References

1. Reznik, A., et al.: Developing software for multi-access edge computing. ETSI White Paper No. 20, September 2017
2. Armbrust, M., et al.: Above the clouds: a Berkeley view of cloud computing. Technical report (UCB/EECS-2009-28) (2009)
3. Bahreini, T., Grosu, D.: Efficient placement of multi-component applications in edge computing systems. In: Proceedings of the Second ACM/IEEE Symposium on Edge Computing, SEC 2017, pp. 5:1–5:11. ACM, New York (2017)
4. Bonomi, F., Milito, R., Zhu, J., Addepalli, S.: Fog computing and its role in the internet of things. In: Proceedings of the First Edition of the MCC Workshop on Mobile Cloud Computing, MCC 2012, pp. 13–16. ACM, New York (2012)
5. Fatima, I., Javaid, N., Nadeem Iqbal, M., Shafi, I., Anjum, A., Ullah Memon, U.: Integration of cloud and fog based environment for effective resource distribution in smart buildings. In: 2018 14th International Wireless Communications Mobile Computing Conference (IWCMC), pp. 60–64, June 2018
6. Givehchi, O., Imtiaz, J., Trsek, H., Jasperneite, J.: Control-as-a-service from the cloud: a case study for using virtualized PLCs. In: 2014 10th IEEE Workshop on Factory Communication Systems (WFCS), pp. 1–4, May 2014

---

[8] https://aws.amazon.com/fargate/.

7. Gu, L., Zeng, D., Guo, S., Barnawi, A., Xiang, Y.: Cost efficient resource management in fog computing supported medical cyber-physical system. IEEE Trans. Emerg. Top. Comput. **5**(1), 108–119 (2017)
8. Gupta, H., Dastjerdi, A., Ghosh, S., Buyya, R.: iFogSim: a toolkit for modeling and simulation of resource management techniques in internet of things, edge and fog computing environments. Softw. Pract. Experience **47**(9), 1275–1296 (2017)
9. Hegazy, T., Hefeeda, M.: Industrial automation as a cloud service. IEEE Trans. Parallel Distrib. Syst. **PP**(99), 1 (2014)
10. IEC: Service diagnostic interface for consumer electronics products and networks. IEC 62394 (2017)
11. IEC: Communication networks and systems for power utility automation. IEC 61850 (2020)
12. Mechalikh, C., Taktak, H., Moussa, F.: Pureedgesim: a simulation toolkit for performance evaluation of cloud, fog, and pure edge computing environments, July 2019
13. Naina, P.M., Rajamani, H., Swarup, K.S.: Modeling and simulation of virtual power plant in energy management system applications. In: 2017 7th International Conference on Power Systems (ICPS), pp. 392–397, December 2017
14. Orsini, G., Bade, D., Lamersdorf, W.: Cloudaware: a context-adaptive middleware for mobile edge and cloud computing applications. In: 2016 IEEE 1st International Workshops on Foundations and Applications of Self* Systems (FAS*W), pp. 216–221, September 2016
15. Pallasch, C., et al.: Edge powered industrial control: concept for combining cloud and automation technologies. In: 2018 IEEE International Conference on Edge Computing (EDGE), pp. 130–134, July 2018
16. Ren, J., Yu, G., Cai, Y., He, Y.: Latency optimization for resource allocation in mobile-edge computation offloading. IEEE Trans. Wirel. Commun. **17**(8), 5506–5519 (2018)
17. Ren, J., Yu, G., He, Y., Li, G.Y.: Collaborative cloud and edge computing for latency minimization. IEEE Trans. Veh. Technol. **68**(5), 5031–5044 (2019)
18. Skarin, P., Tärneberg, W., Årzen, K., Kihl, M.: Towards mission-critical control at the edge and over 5G. In: 2018 IEEE International Conference on Edge Computing (EDGE), pp. 50–57, July 2018
19. Song, Y., Yau, S.S., Yu, R., Zhang, X., Xue, G.: An approach to QoS-based task distribution in edge computing networks for IoT applications. In: 2017 IEEE International Conference on Edge Computing (EDGE), pp. 32–39, June 2017
20. Sonmez, C., Ozgovde, A., Ersoy, C.: Edgecloudsim: An environment for performance evaluation of edge computing systems. In: 2017 Second International Conference on Fog and Mobile Edge Computing (FMEC), pp. 39–44, May 2017
21. Xia, Y.: Cloud control systems. IEEE/CAA J. Automatica Sin. **2**(2), 134–142 (2015)
22. Zhang, Y., Liang, K., Zhang, S., He, Y.: Applications of edge computing in PIoT. In: 2017 IEEE Conference on Energy Internet and Energy System Integration (EI2), pp. 1–4, November 2017

Edge Architecture for Dynamic Data Stream Analysis and Manipulation

Orpaz Goldstein[1,2](✉), Anant Shah[2](✉), Derek Shiell[2](✉),
Mehrdad Arshad Rad[2](✉), William Pressly[2](✉), and Majid Sarrafzadeh[1](✉)

[1] University of California Los Angeles, Los Angeles, USA
{orpgol,majid}@cs.ucla.edu
[2] Verizon Digital Media, Los Angeles, USA
{anant.shah,derek.shiell,mehrdad.radmehrdad.rad,
william.pressly}@verizondigitalmedia.com

Abstract. The exponential growth in IoT and connected devices featuring limited computational capabilities requires the delegation of computation tasks to cloud compute platforms. Edge compute tasks largely involve sending data from an edge compute device to a central location where data is processed and returned to the edge device as a response. Since most edge network infrastructure is restricted in its ability to dynamically delegate computation while retaining context, these events are commonly limited to a predefined task that the edge function is modeled to process and respond to. Edge functions traditionally handle isolated events or periodic updates, making them ill-suited for continuous tasks on streaming data. We propose a decentralized, massively scalable architecture of modular edge compute components which dynamically defines computation channels in the network, with emphasis on the ability to efficiently process data streams from a large amount of producers and support a large amount of consumers in real time. We test this architecture on real-world tasks, involving chaining of edge functions, context retention, and machine learning models on the edge, demonstrating its viability.

1 Introduction

The recent proliferation of IoT devices has been complemented by the rapidly increasing development of serverless ecosystems, in addition to a variety of architectures for managing the complexity of pervasive IoT [1,2].

As we connect more and more internet dependent devices that require continuous, low latency connection to the network, congestion on centralized cloud servers and increasing bandwidth requirements have pushed the creation of the edge network paradigm. The edge in all its variations, moves the previously centralized services to a physically closer location to the end user. Operating on the edge of a network in this way, allows for a decentralized approach that greatly benefits its users in 4 distinct areas: Increasing bandwidth and responsiveness, high scalability, increased privacy using local policies, and outage mitigation [3].

© Springer Nature Switzerland AG 2020
A. Katangur et al. (Eds.): EDGE 2020, LNCS 12407, pp. 33–49, 2020.
https://doi.org/10.1007/978-3-030-59824-2_3

Multi-access edge computing (MEC) is an example of an edge network architecture in active deployment stages that is gaining popularity [4]. MEC utilizes available infrastructure used for radio access networks (RAN), and adds computation and storage capabilities to nodes that are already physically close to end users. In order to control latency and bandwidth on access to these nodes, MEC is expected to be paired with emerging 5G technologies to support traffic to nodes. While operating on the edge of the network, MEC support for computation delegation is usually passed to centralized cloud services, although to much lesser extent than current computation delegation [5]. In most cases MEC makes up the gateway access to a providers core network services that are physically further away in the hierarchy of the edge/cloud network. Effective use of MEC still requires an intermediate layer, closer than a central cloud. One possible approach then could be pairing MEC as a first layer of access to a larger edge network.

In the serverless world, the idea of functions as a service (FaaS) is rapidly becoming the preferred solution for IoT use-cases. Typically, serverless functions are of limited expressiveness and are designed to scale, preventing state information from being stored between executions [6]. Data stream related computation delegation is in turn thought of as a rigidly defined task delegation. Unlike standard FaaS usage, we are interested in defining computation paths for pipe-lining execution of edge models and functions, and provide a mechanism to orchestrate this execution and exchange of meta-data between functions and models. Data streams related tasks, such as video augmentation and analysis, might benefit from function chaining while retaining context, with multiple forking of tasks based on slightly different final product requirement of different consumers. Or alternatively, for a consumer who relies on data produced by multiple producers. Another example are context dependent models on the edge. In order to train and test machine learning models delegated to an edge network, context must be retained and potentially shared between locations.

For Example: Imagine a network connected camera that uploads a live video feed to the network. One consumer wants to run a facial recognition model on the feed, and another wants to augment the feed and add bounding boxes to elements in the feed. Each of these consumers is able to define a function/model that directly subscribes to the availability of that video feed frames on the network. Once they are available, each function picks them up and computes a result that is in turn published as available on the network for the original and additional consumers to pick up.

We then wish to retain some contextual information while data is handed off from function to function, and eventually returned to a consumer. Recent work suggests the addition of ephemeral storage for short-lived edge compute tasks to achieve near real-time performance [7]. This fine-grained scalability appears to be key in developing future serverless applications that could both process multiple data streams in parallel and achieve real-time performance. Whether that refers to facial recognition on mobile devices, flying drones, or driving smart cars, support for this computation with low latency is crucial [8]. Additionally, since users of an edge network will be geographically distributed, low latency availability of an edge function should be unbound to a specific location or edge node. Similarly, data produced in one location should be simultaneously available as input to functions and models across all edge nodes.

For Example: If a user is training a facial recognition model on the edge using video feed from a mobile camera that he carries with him, that model should be available with low latency regardless of a user's physical location. If multiple users are training the same type of facial recognition model, it might make sense to share the data stream with all users globally. Conversely, if the data stream is private, we should make each of the mini models available globally and utilize what they learned to minimize training time across the board.

Figure 1 plots our data stream use-cases over a desired edge network architecture, where data produced is globally available, and any edge function/model can utilize output from other functions and continue computation while retaining context.

Our contribution in this paper is multifaceted:

i We maintain edge-level low latency and availability to physically close users, while extending the availability of produced data streams globally with low latency, without going through a centralized location.

ii We extend the definition of computation on an edge network to be more dynamic in nature. Delegated computation or usage of a function or a model that is not on a user's local node should be handed off in-network to potentially multiple locations for added efficiency, instead of reaching a centralized data center. Delegated computation should communicate meta-data back and forth to coordinate.

iii We provide an architecture where a produced data stream, or the output of a model that takes that stream as input, is available to be consumed by multiple consumers globally. Similarly, input to an edge function that depends on multiple data streams produced in various geographical locations is available instantly. Consequently, to support this kind of global availability, a modular approach to computation delegation is considered. Supporting modularity of the edge, manifested in chaining of edge functions and decentralized learning models on an edge network, requires adding context retention to the edge.

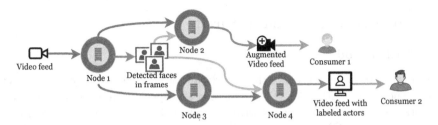

Fig. 1. Red arrows represent the original video input available to edge nodes, yellow arrows are intermediate context being fed along with data, blue arrows are outputs from edge functions/models, and green arrows represent data consumed by an end consumer. This figure shows video feed uploaded to an edge network, where it is ingested by different nodes, each potentially outputs a result that in turn could be again consumed. (Color figure online)

2   Related Work

A lot of recent work that suggests improvement to current edge architecture is centered around reducing latency and increasing efficiency. This could be done by combining the availability and low latency quality of the edge while inheriting the advantages of data center based service delivery [9], or by moving away from a centralized cloud approach to a more decentralized one [10]. On top of that the issue of Quality of Service (QoS) and understanding the benefits of offloading computation within an edge network becomes important when scaling up service to more and more IoT clients. An approach to periodically distribute incoming tasks is described in [11], showing that internally distributing tasks can result in a larger number of tasks processed. [12] extends the notion of offloading computation and computes a delay metric to find the best neighbor node in a network to offload to. Multi-access edge computing (MEC) is surveyed in [13] as a promising target for improving performance of delegated compute to an edge network, and compares different MEC concepts in terms of computation and control placement.

Running models that require state retention on an edge network could be challenging to orchestrate. In the centralized case, federated models were proposed to compute an aggregate of all model updates and broadcast them back to the sub models [14]. However this centralized approach will not work well on streaming data, or generalize to all possible state retaining applications. In the decentralized approach, some work addresses the need for internal communication and passing of information between models. [15] explores the benefits of message passing to compute the same federated aggregation and efficiently compute a decentralized federated model. [16] discusses the treatment of data streams on an edge network for the consumption of learning models. Locality of computation offloading as well as the minimization of raw data routed to a centralized location is highlighted as necessary for overall performance of IoT supporting edge network. Our work in this paper presents a design that adheres to the same decentralized approach, focused on maximizing efficiency in handling data streams from multitude of clients.

3   Proposed Edge Architecture

3.1   Background

A natural candidate to provide the foundation of an edge network is a content delivery network (CDN). A CDN can be seen as a specialized use-case of an edge network, as it is a low latency distributed network in close physical proximity to consumers. A CDN is concerned with caching content as close as possible to end users so it could be consumed by multiple consumers with the least possible latency. Unlike the multi purpose edge network, a CDN does not provide clients with an access point into its network. A CDN does not outsource computation to users as a service or allow them to upload any code to the CDN network. To utilize a CDN as an edge network, low latency edge nodes that allow users access into the larger network are needed, combined with support for requesting compute resources.

3.2   CDN as a Platform for EdgeCompute

We propose an edge network implemented over an existing large commercial content delivery network (CDN). By leveraging an existing global network of points of presence (PoPs) that are deployed in large metro areas around the world, we get physically close to a large portion of the population on the planet. We can then construct a globally available edge presence with exceptionally low latency from outside of the network to edge nodes, as well as internally between our PoPs, from edge node to edge node.

We leverage existing CDN features when extending the network. The CDN is made to handle load balancing of traffic while taking latency into consideration. A CDN has built-in support for routing incoming traffic to the nearest PoP with the capacity to process the request efficiently. Traffic routing and management, as well as fail-overs from PoP to PoP are then taken care of by CDN logic. Since the CDN has a global presence, that translates to low latency hops globally. For an edge network user, that means that while he only maintains a connection with a local edge node, he can still benefit from a low latency global computation delegation. A CDN network has valuable security features in place, such as web application firewall (WAF) and authentication to our network. Further benefits include rate limiting of traffic, and the ability to use the CDN cache when necessary. Inherently, edge compute traffic enjoys the same benefits. Lastly, we make use of a load aware auto-scaling mechanism. On a CDN, when a piece of data becomes popular and frequently requested, it makes sense to replicate that piece of data to more cache servers so it could be served more efficiently from more servers without hurting the performance of the network. The auto-scaling mechanism is used when scaling up our edge compute tasks and as we describe later, when we augment the network with a new kind of data store.

3.3   Extending a CDN

Virtualization. In order to support edge compute on our network and generalize CDN services, we allow users to upload code to be run on our network in a virtualized environment. Allowing each machine to support multiple users operating in isolation on the same hardware resources, we bound models/functions to a user-space container on a machine. The container approach for OS level virtualization of resources is highly scalable, and can be further improved by container orchestration software, automating global management and scaling of containers. Containers are fast and easy to deploy using provided packaging and deployment tools, while allowing for individualized system configuration at deployment time. Containers requires small amount of resources to maintain, and their footprint on a system is minimal. We use Docker as our container platform, and support uploading docker images containing functions or models to be run on our edge network.

Data Store and Context Retention. Unlike the common edge network implementation, the edge functions uploaded by our user do not need to integrate with an http request logic library in order to obtain data as input. Instead, we implement a distributed globally available edge key value store (EKV). Using a persistent, globally distributed data store, provides an edge network with the ability to retain context between function executions, or an online learning model to be updated from multiple nodes around the network. An EKV provides a producer with a low latency access point to upload data streams, after which the data propagates through the edge network quickly to become available globally. Equivalently, consumers are able to access data streams produced remotely, on their local edge node instantly.

Figure 2 shows our CDN based architecture; Global decentralization and low latency availability is key in a network designed for massive scale data stream input. Figure 3 shows our layering scheme and the path of a user request interacting with our network. Requests from the outer layer that is close to a user propagate internally using CDN mechanics augmented with a globally available storage system.

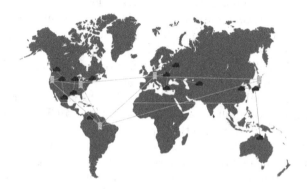

Fig. 2. Edge CDN Architecture. Red connections are strongly consistent database connections. Green connections are edge node to edge node connectivity. Blue connections are edge node to database connections. (Color figure online)

Computation Channels. On the producer side, once data is produced it is pushed to a local edge instance of our EKV. Once uploaded, we wish to notify functions and models who are dependant on this data that a new piece of data is available to be consumed. In order for edge functions or models to become aware of the new data availability, we implement computation channels that are essentially named communication channels that functions or models are able to subscribe to and receive data from. In practice, to let subscribers know when to pull data from the EKV store, a user implements a publish call when a producer has finished uploading data to EKV. This allows functions and models that are subscribed to the computation channel dedicated to the data produced by a specific producer, to get data from EKV and start working. Similarly, an implemented consumer function, model, or end user subscribes to the channel that matches the data they wish to consume.

To create computation channels, we are using the pub/sub paradigm. This approach provides us the scalability and modularity required by our implementation. Although pub/sub has some inherent rigidity as related to modifying published data, our approach allows for flexibility in the definition of EKV keys that are published via our channels. A user might publish multiple data chunks via a single key if he is not concerned about consistency, or publish a new key on every new upload if he is. Data that is augmented by a function is considered new data and is (re)published separately. Using these channels is not limited to passing EKV keys. Computation delegation across different nodes that do not require EKV data store might still use pub/sub channels to exchange meta-data between executions, pass function return values that do not require storage, and coordinate runs across different locations.

To implement computation channels, we selected the MQTT messaging protocol as our message broker. MQTT shares the IoT approach where any device is a potential client, and is flexible in using quality of service (QOS) assurances that tie nicely with a data stream approach. As our MQTT server, we use a Mosquitto broker on our edge nodes. Mosquitto is robust enough to run on our heavy duty servers supporting high volumes of messages, as well as lightweight enough for potentially running on dedicated low power edge hardware.

Figure 4 shows a demo of computational channels for data produced outside the network, and Fig. 5 shows a demo of computational channels for data produced inside the network architecture. The different propagation paths of the data uploaded to the EKV store and the MQTT pub/sub calls are denoted using color arrows. This representation is meant to capture the concurrency of our network and the emphasis of global availability.

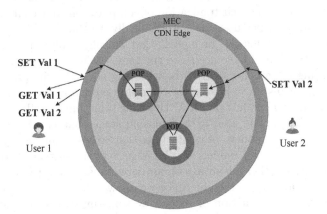

Fig. 3. Edge Architecture layers. Extending current CDN architecture using a global persistent database. MEC outer layer allows low latency edge node computation and access to larger CDN edge network. PoPs and EKV instances are interconnected. A value computed across the network is still available for local consumption.

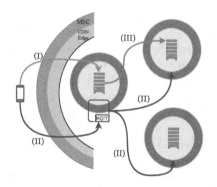
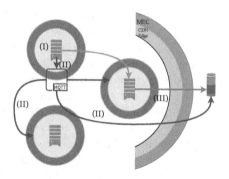

Fig. 4. Computational pathways incoming demo. (i) Smartphone uploads text data (blue arrow) and publishes availability via MQTT broker (green arrow). (ii) MQTT broker forwards the publication (green arrows) and EKV store makes data available to all edge nodes. (iii) Once the subscribed edge function receives MQTT publications, it pulls the text data (red arrow) and runs compute. (Color figure online)

Fig. 5. Computational pathways outgoing demo. (i) An edge function finishes computation, it pushes outputs data to EKV (local so no arrows), followed by a MQTT publish call (green arrows). (ii) Finally a subscribed user receives the publication and requests the data from EKV, which retrieves it from source (blue arrow), and then allows user to pull (red arrow). (Color figure online)

3.4 Resulting Set up and Real World Example

The described set up allows a highly dynamic computation pipeline on the edge. The subscription to computational channels could be as hierarchically complicated as needed, using multiple layers deep of edge computation subscriptions. This allows for fine grained customization of computation that could be in turn individualized up to a per user case. Additionally, this allows for invocation of highly localized edge functions or models that are physically far away, but are on the same network and have access to the same EKV. A motivating example would be sharing a trained model without having access to the private data it was trained on, for instance: if we want to train a model on the edge, we might benefit from utilizing models on EKV that did something similar in different geo-locations. This can be seen as a debiasing stage that is private and edge contained. Federating models prevents bias that arises from locally collected training data, and sharing models on the edge network instead of data keeps that data private. Another advantage of our network is the ability to retain context and make it available globally. Since we allow subscribing to computation results of another edge function or model, we sometimes need to maintain the proper context in addition to the output on EKV.

For Example: Say we are feeding a video to the edge, and a function is subscribed to detect faces in frames of the video feed. The output of that function is the coordinates of a bounding box for a face in the frames. Now, if a function is subscribed to the results of that face detection function and is planning to use the face detection results and continue to augment the faces on these frames, it will need both the coordinates produced by the face detection function in addition to the original frames on EKV. To support such a use-case we need to understand what a subscription to a computational channel depends on. In this case, that subscription to the output of face detection is dependant on the original frames being available in EKV. We solve this by having the augmenting function subscribe to two computational channels and starting work when both a frame and its corresponding coordinates are available. Lastly, all computation is done on the edge whether local or remote. There is no delegation to a centralized cloud. Instead, any non local edge node might potentially participate in computation if such delegation is needed.

Figure 6 and 7 show a demo of a text-to-speech task execution on our architecture. The different propagation paths of the data uploaded to the EKV store and the MQTT pub/sub calls are denoted using color arrows. The latency observed on MQTT publication and data transfers from outside the network to a PoP with an EKV instance, and from EKV to another PoP that had our Text-to-Speech function is denoted on the plot. This representation captures our real world experimentation with our architecture and the latency observed.

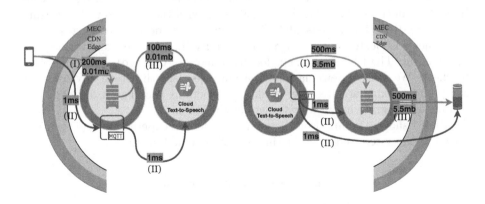

Fig. 6. Text2speech incoming. (i) Smartphone uploads text data (blue arrow) and publishes availability via MQTT broker (green arrow). (ii) MQTT broker forwards the publication (green arrow) and EKV store makes data available to all edge nodes. (iii) Once the subscribed edge function receives MQTT publications, it pulls the text data (red arrow) and runs compute. (Color figure online)

Fig. 7. Text2speech outgoing. (i) Text-to-speech model finishes run, it pushes outputs data to EKV (local so no arrows), followed by a MQTT publish call (green arrows). (ii) Finally a subscribed user receives the publication and requests the data from EKV, which retrieves it from source (blue arrow), and then allows user to pull (red arrow). (Color figure online)

4 Experiments and Measurements

Our architecture is built to support large amounts of data stream traffic and computation paths within the network. We show in our experiments the advantages of our network in a few key edge related tasks. We show how close we can get to real time delivery of results from edge functions and models working on analyzing data streams. We evaluate the efficiency of chaining different functions while retaining meta-data between executions. And we evaluate how close we can get to real time generation of data from a machine learning model, based on ques from a user outside our network. The tasks are as follows:

1. Run an emotion detection (ED) model as an edge function on recorded voice samples from an IoT device and show detected emotion in real time.
2. Run a text to speech (T2S) function on the edge that accepts text from a user and outputs generated human voices that will then be consumed by a second IoT device.
3. Pipeline 3 image related machine learning model that will accept as input a video stream and output an augmented version of it (DF).

For each of these we report all metrics relating to latency and connectivity throughout the path of execution. All experiments were run on our 32 core Intel(R) Xeon(R) Gold 6140 CPU @ 2.30 GHz, with the last two tasks utilizing a single 8 GB NVIDIA Tesla M60 GPU. The edge node we are using in these experiments is located in close physical proximity (Los Angeles) and within 5 ms to the client. The EKV instance is located remotely (Chicago) and within 7 ms to client. We show a few machine learning use-cases that take advantage of our proposed edge architecture. Models or functions running on our edge can seamlessly integrate into a user's edge function chain.

Table 1 shows a comparisons between the different experiments and their key points we are interested in evaluating on our edge architecture.

Table 1. Experiment Comparison

	ED	T2S	DF
Pub/Sub	✓	✓	✓
EKV Data Store	×	✓	✓
Function chaining	×	×	✓
Small files incoming	✓	✓	×
Small files outgoing	✓	✓	×
Large files incoming	×	×	✓
Large files outgoing	×	✓	✓
Model is target specific	×	×	✓

4.1   Emotion Detection from Voice Samples

With the expanding array of smart speakers consumers interact with, voice analysis becomes a common task for extracting commands, as well as features from voice that are unrelated to the spoken text. Here, we evaluate here the usage of a machine learning model trained to classify positive and negative emotions on the edge and return a response in real time. This task shows low latency availability of our emotion detection model, and utilization of computation channels to exchange small amounts of data and coordinate execution.

Using a database of labeled actor voices emulating emotions, we pre-train our model and package it into a Docker container deployed on the edge. The dataset we used is described in [17]. We create two MQTT channels. One for incoming data and one for outgoing classification. We then create and subscribe an edge function that listens to incoming publications and branch an instance of the emotion detection model for each incoming request. On the client side, we create a web page for recording voice samples using JavaScript, and use paho-mqtt in the browser to subscribe to the channels for this process. The voice samples are recorded trough the browser, serialized and sent through MQTT as the payload of the MQTT publish call. The edge function receives the serialized file, passes it to the emotion detection model, and publishes the classification results via MQTT. The browser then receives the publication and displays an emoticon on screen.[1] The voice sample size depends on the recording length, but we have found that a file of about 100 kb could be published via MQTT and received by the listener function in less than 3 ms. After the function loads the pre-trained model and passes the data, the model takes about 4.5 s to run using only the CPUs on the edge node. The model output is then published back received by the client after another 2 ms and finally the client displays an emoticon after about 4.5 s from the end of the recording process.

As a comparison, we consider a standard cloud architecture, with serverless functions that accept data via HTTP requests. The ping to an average cloud instance takes an average of 224 ms[2], and response time per message using HTTP is 200 ms higher than that of MQTT when connection is reused.[3] Including the time it will take to move the data makes our task potentially 1–3 s longer on public cloud. A significant user impact.

4.2   Text to Speech

Offloading the resource intense process of data generation using a relatively small amount of data is another area where edge networks shine. Asking an edge node to generate images for us using a description, or generated human voice from raw text are only two examples, out of which we will examine the latter here. This task shows a producer and consumer that are operating independently in

---

[1] A video showing the emotion detection task can be seen here.

[2] Measured using 'curl' to 30 public cloud instances from different companies and averaged.

[3] Detailed comparison can be seen here.

different locations using different edge nodes for EKV and edge function. The edge nodes used are in Chicago and California and are 1 ms apart when using ping.

Using a model based on Deep Voice 3 [18], we create an edge function that is able to receive a blob of raw text and parameters indicating what kind of speaker the model should generate, and outputs a recording of human voice that speaks the text that was received. We create two MQTT channels, one for publishing blobs of text, and the other for publishing human voices. Our edge function subscribes to the text channel, and waits for a publication that a new blob of text is available on EKV along with the parameters of what voice should be generated. An instance of our function starts for each blob/speaker pair. We create a producer of text that pushes text to EKV and publishes on the text channel, and a separate consumer that subscribes to both channels and consumes both the text and the corresponding human voice that our edge function outputs. This simulates a situation where the producer is not the final destination for the processing result on the produced data. We run the producer and consumer in separate locations, and time the task of a producer pushing a blob of text and asks for 10 different human voices generated for each blob. The producer pushes approximately 200 bytes of text to EKV and receives confirmation within 200 ms, once the data is on EKV the producer publishes via MQTT that a new blob is ready for consumption. The edge function pulls the text from EKV and starts 10 instances of text to speech translation after about 500 ms. The consumer receives the publication and prints out the text after 250 ms of process start. The edge text to speech function outputs 10 .WAV files weighing a total of 5.8 Mb after working for 4 s. It then uploads them to EKV simultaneously and receives a final confirmation from EKV after a total of 5.5 s from process start. The function then publishes to MQTT the availability of results. Once the consumer receives the publication of new available data, it pulls the data from EKV and saves them locally after about 6.3 s from process start.[4]

To compare, we look at the average latency between nodes of popular cloud services.[5] In addition to the 224 ms average ping time from client to cloud service and 200 ms longer response time per message, average latency between public cloud nodes is approximately 160 ms. Depending on implementation of storage and upload/download of data, our task will take at best seconds longer on the average public cloud.

4.3   Video Stream Manipulation

Leveraging the edge as a live video manipulation tool opens the doors for many interesting use-cases such as dynamically augmented video streams. Combining that with machine learning models such as Deepfake, lets us imagine a future where we consume personally tailored video streams, replacing actors in a movie we are watching on the fly. We will examine how we can use our architecture,

---

[4] A video showing the text to speech task can be seen here.

[5] latency average was computed based on information in: https://www.cloudping.co/.

and create a pipeline of functions to create a augmented version of a video stream as close to real time as possible. This task evaluates chaining of functions and models to augment a video feed live. Producer and consumer are operating independently in different locations using different edge nodes for EKV and edge function. The edge nodes used are in Chicago and California and are 1 ms apart when using ping.

We define 4 computation channels. We have an edge function and two edge models chained, each subscribed to the output of the previous functions, and an extra channel publishing the availability of the original frames on EKV that all are subscribed to, thus creating a pipeline of computation for the video frames to go through. We also define a helper edge function that extracts individual frames from a video clip using FFMPEG library.[6]

(i) Face Detection. First, we have a function based on OpenCV face detection that accepts video frames as input and outputs location of faces in frames. Once a frame is passed to the function it is passed to OpenCV where frames are rotated and scaled multiple times as the OpenCV detector function scans for faces. Coordinates for detected faces are saved on EKV.

(ii) Face Classification. Coordinates for faces that are identified by the previous function as well as the original frames are ingested by a model based on VGG face classification [19] pre-trained for face classification using 2.6 M images from 2622 identities. Our model is used to identify a specific face of interest that we wish to augment. It accepts a frame with a face and a reference image, and outputs whether the face in the frame matches our person of interest back to EKV.

(iii) Face Augmentation. Frames that were marked by the classification model are then picked up by our Deepfake model that is based on work of [20]. The model uses the stored coordinates for each frame to extract a cropped face to convert. The model then performs conversion of the frame, reconstructed to fake the source face in the original frame into the desired target face, and output the augmented frames back to EKV.

Data used for training of our model has been scraped from YouTube videos of the original source face and the target face, and in total used to create around 5000 images of each. The model is trained by us for one week using a single NVIDIA Tesla M60 GPU before compiled as an edge function.

(iv) Consumer. A consumer that is subscribed to the original stream in addition to the output of the deepfake function, is able to pick up the video feed with augmented frames from EKV and view the feed locally.

---

[6] A video showing the augmentation task can be seen here.

Timing. The producer streams 20 s chunks of video to EKV weighing an average of 1.9 Mb. A single chunk takes about 300 ms to upload to EKV and receive confirmation for. The producer then publishes via MQTT that the chunk is ready for consumption. Face detection then picks up the chunk and starts the process of detecting faces. Coordinates of each face detected is immediately pushed to EKV and published as available. The first video chunk takes about 36 s to process due to model loading, and each following chunk will be processed within 300 ms of producer pushing to EKV. Face classification receives publication and within less then 20 ms classifies the face pushes result to EKV and publishes availability. The face augmentation phase then has received publications from all channels it is subscribed to and starts working on changing the faces on a chunk of video. Converting the entire 20 s chunk of video takes 18 s. The Deepfake model than pushes changed frame back to EKV and publishes availability within a few milliseconds. Lastly, the consumer receives the publication of availability of frames. Once there is a 20 s chunk of frames available, it uses the helper function to convert them back into a video file, downloads and plays them. From publication of faked frames, it takes the consumer approximately 500 ms to convert and download the 20 s chunk of video. Overall for the first chunk, it takes about 55 s for a chunk of video to be augmented and viewed on the consumer end. After the first chunk it will take under 20 s for the entire pipeline to finish working on a 20 s chunk. We then can keep our augmented video feed about 1 min behind live video.

Comparing to the latency on a public cloud service, In addition to the 224 ms average ping time from client to cloud service and 200 ms longer response time per message, and an average of 160 ms latency between distant nodes, we add the accumulating latency of making the intermediate results of each function globally available for consumption. Assuming data passes via http/https, our task could not be augmented fast enough to be viewed in pseudo-live time.

5   Conclusion

In this paper we have examined the recent development in edge network design, as well as the role of the edge network for the near future connectivity requirements, and have proposed an architecture to close that gap. By building our edge network on top of an existing CDN and extending it, we have constructed a massively scalable edge network. We have demonstrated the benefits of having both computational paths that can operate as meta-data exchange channels for coordination or limited size message passing. And the benefit of having a globally connected data store for context retention and intermediate data storage where learning models can read and write to and keep a global low latency availability. Demonstrating the above, we have provided 3 real world machine learning tasks making use of computation paths and context and data retention.

A   Comparison with different architectures

In addition to the benefits accrued by our overarching edge architecture, there is room to break down individual components and compare them to other possible design choices. MQTT is one protocol chosen from the few emerging protocols of choice for the IoT world. While we evaluated both MQTT and CoAP and found both to be comparable, we chose MQTT for our pub/sub protocol as it had better library availability and broker seleciton. We compare our choice of MQTT with an HTTP based singnaling mechanism to support our architecture. In our architecture, we make use of MQTT as a signaling channel between subscribed clients waiting on streams of data, and between edge nodes coordinating execution of models on data. The key observation here is that our MQTT connection are seldom closed, and in most cases reused many times between the time they are established and close. The comparison made in [21] clearly shows the benefits of utilizing an open MQTT connection with exponential benefits over the same use case implemented using HTTP. Similarly to [21], we investigate the difference between 1, 10, and 100 messages each weighing 10 bytes, transmitted over MQTT and HTTP, over 10 trials. This simulates transferring simple instructions and EKV data locations in our computation channels. For MQTT we connect once and reuse the same connection to communicate all subsequent messages. For HTTP we use POST requests. All communication was evaluated between an edge node and a local client, emulating a real world scenario. Figure 8 and 9 show the log scale results for speed in ms, as observed in our test. Since HTTP grows as a factor of messages passed we see the benefit of opening a single MQTT connection to be used over multiple messages.

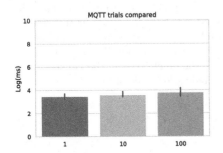
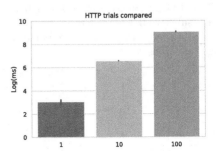

Fig. 8. MQTT speed per number of requests compared at log scale of ms.

Fig. 9. HTTP speed per number of requests compared at log scale of ms.

Another aspect worthy of comparison is the speed gain of using our architecture as compared to the same job implemented as a FAAS workflow, where results must be returned back to a user before the next function in a pipeline is started. We compare a simple numpy matrix multiplication task, called via our MQTT computation channels 1,10 and 100 times, where results are pushed to a MinIO storage instance. This is compared to the case where a function runs and returns a result directly to a client. In the case where we run our function more than 1 time, we compute the next result based on the previous functions result. In the FAAS like use case, the client sends back the result to the function, and in our architecture, the previous result is picked up from our MinIO instance. Figures 10 and 11 show the comparison between the two approaches. It can be seen that the impact on sending the little amount of data we use back and forth using HTTP POST requests, essentially does not change the POST requests time for execution. While the time increases using MQTT computation channels and ephemeral storage, where an extra call to the MinIO server is needed. However, even with this increase, it can be seen that as the amount of concurrent requests grow, the penalty incurred by POST requests is far more inhibiting then the extra hop to MinIO. As we have previously shown in our experiments, MQTT can be used for small scale data and speed up computation even more in cased where not much data is moved in the network.

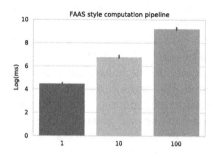
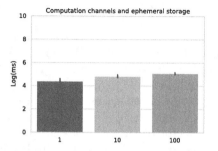

Fig. 10. Speed of calling our function via HTTP POST requests, and sending back the result for all cases where the function was called more than once. Compared at log scale of ms.

Fig. 11. Speed of calling our function via an MQTT computation channel, send result to an ephemeral storage, and compute results based on previous function run for all cases where we call the function more than once. Compared at log scale of ms.

References

1. Lucero, S., et al.: IoT platforms: enabling the internet of things. White paper (2016)
2. Shi, W., Dustdar, S.: The promise of edge computing. Computer **49**(5), 78–81 (2016)
3. Satyanarayanan, M.: The emergence of edge computing. Computer **50**(1), 30–39 (2017)
4. Multi-access-edge computing. https://www.etsi.org/technologies/multi-access-edge-computing

5. Taleb, T., Samdanis, K., Mada, B., Flinck, H., Dutta, S., Sabella, D.: On multi-access edge computing: a survey of the emerging 5G network edge cloud architecture and orchestration. IEEE Commun. Surv. Tutorials **19**(3), 1657–1681 (2017)
6. Baldini, I., et al.: Serverless computing: current trends and open problems. In: Chaudhary, S., Somani, G., Buyya, R. (eds.) Research Advances in Cloud Computing, pp. 1–20. Springer, Singapore (2017). https://doi.org/10.1007/978-981-10-5026-8_1
7. Klimovic, A., Wang, Y., Stuedi, P., Trivedi, A., Pfefferle, J., Kozyrakis, C.: Pocket: elastic ephemeral storage for serverless analytics. In: 13th USENIX Symposium on Operating Systems Design and Implementation, OSDI 2018, pp. 427–444 (2018)
8. Shi, W., Cao, J., Zhang, Q., Li, Y., Xu, L.: Edge computing: vision and challenges. IEEE Internet Things J. **3**(5), 637–646 (2016)
9. Chang, H., Hari, A., Mukherjee, S., Lakshman, T.: Bringing the cloud to the edge. In: 2014 IEEE Conference on Computer Communications Workshops (INFOCOM WKSHPS), pp. 346–351. IEEE (2014)
10. Garcia Lopez, P., et al.: Edge-centric computing: vision and challenges (2015)
11. Song, Y., Yau, S.S., Yu, R., Zhang, X., Xue, G.: An approach to QoS-based task distribution in edge computing networks for IoT applications. In: 2017 IEEE International Conference on Edge Computing (EDGE), pp. 32–39. IEEE (2017)
12. Yousefpour, A., Ishigaki, G., Jue, J.P.: Fog computing: towards minimizing delay in the internet of things. In: 2017 IEEE International Conference on Edge Computing (EDGE), pp. 17–24. IEEE (2017)
13. Mach, P., Becvar, Z.: Mobile edge computing: a survey on architecture and computation offloading. IEEE Commun. Surv. Tutorials **19**(3), 1628–1656 (2017)
14. Konečný, J., McMahan, H.B., Yu, F.X., Richtárik, P., Suresh, A.T., Bacon, D.: Federated learning: strategies for improving communication efficiency. arXiv preprint arXiv:1610.05492 (2016)
15. Wang, S., et al.: Adaptive federated learning in resource constrained edge computing systems. IEEE J. Sel. Areas Commun. **37**(6), 1205–1221 (2019)
16. Mohammadi, M., Al-Fuqaha, A., Sorour, S., Guizani, M.: Deep learning for IoT big data and streaming analytics: a survey. IEEE Commun. Surv. Tutorials **20**(4), 2923–2960 (2018)
17. Livingstone, S.R., Russo, F.A.: The Ryerson audio-visual database of emotional speech and song (RAVDESS): a dynamic, multimodal set of facial and vocal expressions in North American English. PLoS ONE **13**(5), e0196391 (2018)
18. Ping, W., et al.: Deep voice 3: scaling text-to-speech with convolutional sequence learning. arXiv preprint arXiv:1710.07654 (2017)
19. Parkhi, O.M., Vedaldi, A., Zisserman, A., et al.: Deep face recognition. In: BMVC, vol. 1, p. 6 (2015)
20. Pu, Y., et al.: Variational autoencoder for deep learning of images, labels and captions. In: Advances in Neural Information Processing Systems, pp. 2352–2360 (2016)
21. Wang, C.: HTTP vs. MQTT: a tale of two IoT protocols (2018)

fogcached: DRAM-NVM Hybrid Memory-Based KVS Server for Edge Computing

Kouki Ozawa[1], Takahiro Hirofuchi[2], Ryousei Takano[2], and Midori Sugaya[1]([⊠])

[1] College of Engineering, Shibaura Institute of Technology, 3-7-5 Toyosu, Koto City,
Tokyo, Japan
doly@shibaura-it.ac.jp
[2] National Institute of Advanced Industrial Science and Technology, 17, Tsukuba 69121, Japan

Abstract. With the widespread use of sensors in smart devices and robots, there is a growing expectation for edge computing that processes data not on distant cloud servers but also on or near interactive devices to store their data with low latency access. To satisfy these requirements, we consider a new edge computing system that consists of a hybrid main memory with a KVS (Key-Value-Store) server utilizing the DRAM and nonvolatile main memory (NVM). It provides large-capacity cache memory in a server, supporting high-speed processing and quick response for sensor nodes. However, since existing KVS servers are not designed for NVM, there are less satisfactory implementations that achieve low response time and high throughputs. We propose a novel hybrid KVS server that is designed and implemented on the Memcached distributed memory-caching system, which dynamically moves cached data between two types of memory devices according to access frequency in order to achieve a low latency compared to the existent approaches. We developed a Dual-LRU (Least Recently Used) structure for it. Evaluation was performed using a real machine equipped with NVM. The result showed the proposed method successfully reduced the response time and improves access throughputs.

Keywords: fogcached · Memcached · NVMM · NVM · DCPM · Dual-LRU · KVS

1 Introduction

With the development of the Internet of Things (IoT) technology, a large amount of data from smart devices and sensors has been transferred to servers. If IoT technology spreads to all parts of our lives in the future, data processing will be required even at the edge near the user [1]. The purpose of the current cloud is to use the resources of geographically separated cloud servers. For this reason, services that allow the effects of delays are mainly configured (Fig. 1). In order to avoid the network delay, it is difficult to send large amounts of data to the remote cloud server. It limits the IoT connected devices. For example, if a robot, which is one of the IoT devices, drives autonomously, it is necessary to process a large amount of image data since generally it collects the information about

A. Katangur et al. (Eds.): EDGE 2020, LNCS 12407, pp. 50–62, 2020.
https://doi.org/10.1007/978-3-030-59824-2_4

the environment, and from that information, makes a map that projects real objects, and the robot calculates the correct trajectory past the objects. To consider to apply the practical uses of the multiple robots, the high-performance response to the large amount of data processing and calculations is necessary for achieving the purpose. Moreover, it is required to drive without a cable so it can move freely, so it is necessary to use wireless communications for the servers without the delay. In such a case, a short-range, low-latency edge cache server is more practical instead of the cloud (Fig. 2).

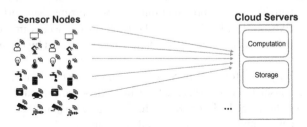

Fig. 1. Existent sensor and cloud server

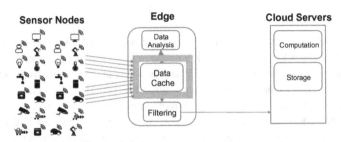

Fig. 2. Required sensor and edge/cloud communication

Based on the recognition, it is indispensable to have a large-capacity, low-latency edge cache server on the premise that service handling and actual conditions are close and large amounts of data are collected by short-range wireless communication. However, such an edge server has not been realized yet.

We focused on a key-value-store (KVS) server that allows temporary caching of large amounts of data. To achieve low latency access to the data, it is desirable for the KVS server to have a large amount of memory. However, the capacity of DRAM currently used as main memory is small, and it is unlikely that it will increase significantly in the future [2]. DRAM is volatile, and its contents are lost if the power supply from outside is interrupted. The edge server can store a large amount of data by using a nonvolatile main memory (NVM), which has the characteristics of being larger and more nonvolatile than DRAM. However, while NVM provides larger capacity than DRAM, its read/write performance is inferior to DRAM. For example, Optane DCPM is presented [3]. The read latency of Optane DCPM is about 3 to 2 times slower than DRAM [4]. In KVS servers, it is necessary to increase the cache hit rate by expanding the capacity of the main memory using NVM, while avoiding performance degradation due to DCPM, which is slower than DRAM.

In this paper, for the typical in-memory KVS Memcached [5], cache data is dynamically moved from DCPM to DRAM according to the access frequency to achieve high-speed response based on general-purpose LRU. As a result, we developed a hybrid main memory system that can respond at high speed by increasing access to faster DRAM while keeping the benefits of the large capacity of cache. In this study, we presented the issues and proposal that satisfy the requirement of the edge computing. We designed and developed a Dual-LRU mechanism on the KVS Memcached. We executed an evaluation experiment using an Optane DCPM and confirmed the basic performance of the proposed mechanism. The result show that our proposed mechanism performed better than the existing Extstore [6], by 40%, and the result of the access improved by five times. We confirmed that performance degradation can be avoided by optimizing cache data.

The paper organized as follows: In Sect. 2 we introduce the related work, Sect. 3 issues and the proposal for our research, then in Sect. 4 we present the design and implementation of the Dual-LRU on KVS. In Sect. 5, we show the conditions and results of the evaluation, and finally we conclude the paper.

2 Related Work

KVS has a well-known mechanism and has been researched a lot. First, we describe conventional NVM KVS research. In KVS systems, persistence has been ensured on many systems using flash storage. In contrast, Fei Xia et al. proposed HiKV, which uses NVM instead of flash storage to guarantee durability [7]. HiKV provides high-speed writing while improving the reliability of metadata. The purpose was to maintain it. However, HiKV Memcached does not support SCAN processing, and HiKV needs to develop B + -Tree independently in the data storage part separately from the conventional Memcached mechanism.

Hao Liu et al. proposed LibreKV [8]. LibreKV has a hash table for both DRAM and NVM in order to respond quickly to requests from clients. When the DRAM hash table is full, it merges with the hash table in NVM. This guarantees high-speed processing of client requests and data persistence. However, LibreKV has a strong role as a database, unlike KVS which has a strong role as a cache such as Memcached. For this reason, there is no mechanism that removes objects from memory when memory is fully used like the LRU of Memcached. This is because it is assumed that the size of the data to be saved is smaller than the memory size of the server. In this study, since the server is assumed to be used as a cache, an LRU-like structure is indispensable.

Wu et al. proposed NVMcached [9]. In NVMcached, the conventional technology for maintaining consistency such as copy-on-write and journaling is a heavy process in applications requiring high-speed processing such as KVS. Therefore, Wu et al. consider the NVM write durability in NVMcached. In their proposed method, they store the list of objects (metadata) in DRAM, and the objects themselves are stored in NVM. Objects that are deleted or updated in a short time in consideration of write endurance are stored in DRAM, rebuilding the list using the objects stored in NVM after the crash. It aimed to achieve both performance and reliability by guaranteeing object persistence with NVM, while speeding up the processing of metadata with DRAM. The above three studies focus on the non-volatility of NVM and are designed to take advantage of reliability, data consistency, and persistence. These commonly consider the place of objects on the different memory devices, and way to access the memory devices. There are no studies that focus on the difference in access speeds of memory devices and examine the maximization of the overall performance of a KVS system.

On the other hand, similar to our research, a study on data management in a hybrid memory using DRAM and NVM has been proposed. Hai Jin and colleagues proposed HMCached [10], which focused on the object placement for the efficient handling of hybrid memory. Hai Jin et al. adopted the multi-queue algorithm [11] as a replacement algorithm that determines which objects are saved when the objects are stored or evicted from DRAM, while following the structure of Memcached. This aims to improve the parallelism in moving objects between DRAM and NVM. The objects stored in NVM were managed by the clock algorithm [12]. This was aimed at saving memory space and avoiding the frequent replacement of doubly linked lists in LRU. Hai Jin et al. set up an access counter for objects and move objects whose access count is greater than or equal to a threshold from NVM to DRAM. In our study, the proposed method in this study follows the segment LRU of Memcached, and can coexist with Extstore, a Memcached function that extends the server using existing storage that is also used in EVcache [13], a cache solution.

Wu [14] proposed that task-based programming, which automatically move the memory pages of a task between memory devices to a hybrid type memory. A similar type of task is analyzed from the information of the task metadata. We implemented a mechanism to analyze the access pattern for a task and automatically move memory pages of the similar types of tasks from NVM to DRAM based on frequently accessed task information. However, since the access patterns in the database can vary greatly from object to object and from time to time, it is difficult to predict the behavior of another similar type of object by analyzing the object in advance, so a design that matches KVS is required.

One of the existent implementations is ex-store, which is an extension function for external storage of Memcached [6]. The ex-store is introduced in EVCache, which is a distributed in-memory caching solution that offloads memory using SSD and non-volatile memory devices [13]. However, since it is assumed that a storage whose access performance is much lower than that of memory is used, there is a problem that the performance of DCPM that can be accessed at a speed comparable to that of DRAM cannot be maximized.

3 Issues and Proposal

3.1 Issues

The existing KVS server extended using the NVM was used as a database that needed to reliably store data. However, we focus on the role of a new cache server for the edge node between the local IoT devices and cloud. The responsibility of the cache highly required. Based on the requirement, we consider the satisfactory algorithm and mechanism. In a hybrid main memory composed of both DRAM and NVM, it is an issue to use both memory devices properly. NVM offers greater capacity than DRAM, however its read()/write() performance is inferior to DRAM. In KVS servers, it is necessary to expand the capacity of the main memory using NVM to increase the hit rate for cached data, while avoiding performance degradation due to NVM, which is slower than DRAM. Currently, the access to the objects on the KVS server is expected to change on each object and vary from time to time. Therefore, it is difficult to determine in advance which object should be stored in high-speed DRAM, and a general-purpose mechanism that dynamically moves the object according to the access to the object is necessary. Intel CPUs that support Optane DCPM are equipped with a function (DCPM memory mode) to use both memory devices properly in the memory controller, however they are low in versatility because they are implemented at the hardware level.

On the other hand, Memcached already has Extstore, a function that retains data using storage in addition to DRAM. However, the design is for flash storage, which is much slower than DRAM at buffering in read()/write() waiting buffers. NVM can be accessed as main memory like DRAM, and it is expected that Memcached's storage utilization function will not be able to bring out sufficient performance for NVM which is larger than DRAM, and the lower latency than storage. We consider a new mechanism compatible with NVM is required.

3.2 Proposal

To satisfy the requirements, we propose a KVS server for hybrid main memory consisting of both DRAM and NVM. For the KVS, we use Memcached, which is a distributed memory cache system that provides the simple mechanism and is commonly used in reliable web servers. It has already provided the mechanism to treat the storage, however, it assumes use of it for the slower disks or the disks that have access speeds worse than the NVM. We consider it is not possible to maximize the performance of DCPM treated as memory. To consider the extension of Memcached, we consider how to extend the segment LRU (Least Recently Used) algorithm, which is implemented on the Memcached. Since the algorithm provides the mechanism to discard the least recently used data first as the backend mechanism, we can concentrate on extending the DRAM to manage the DCPM within the mechanism.

We focus on providing a mechanism for dynamically moving items in two types of memory depending on the access frequency of the items. Maintaining the items with high access in high-speed DRAM and items with low access in low-speed DCPM allows large-capacity data to be retained while mitigating the performance degradation caused by using DCPM that is slower than DRAM.

4 Design and Implementation

4.1 Abstract

We propose an extended KVS server for a hybrid main memory consisting of both DRAM and NVM. Firstly, we analyze the memory management structure of Memcached, and how to extend the structure that can be suitable for the hybrid main memory mechanism. For Memcached, the segment LRU, a memory management mechanism, has been extended to provide a mechanism for dynamically moving items in two types of memory depending on the access frequency of the items. Maintaining frequently accessed the items in a fast memory (DRAM) and the less frequently-accessed items with a slower memory (DCPM) that allows large-capacity data to be retained while mitigating the performance degradation caused by using the slower memory.

4.2 Memcached Slab Class Structure

Before explaining specific design contents, we describe the outline of the structure of Memcached based on this design. It is designed with simple multi-threading. The left-hand picture in Fig. 3 Left shows the Memcached operation of the client and server. It firstly receives the key and value from the client, the worker thread in the server that receives it, and stores the hash value of the key in the hash table of (1). Next, the set of keys, values, and metadata items are stored in the memory of (2). The memory size used by the server is specified when the server starts.

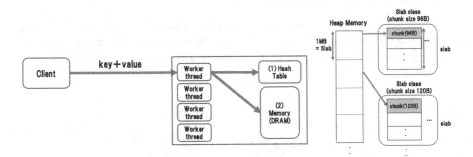

Fig. 3. KVS Memcached communication (left), slab structure (right)

Next, we describe the memory management structure of Memcached, which was the basis of the hybrid memory management structure. As shown in the right Fig. 3, Memcached manages their memory in 1 MB units. 1 MB allocated from memory is called a slab. The slab is further divided into chunks. Slabs are classified by chunk size. For example, a slab with a chunk size of 96 Bbytes is managed as Class 1. Items that are a collection of a key, its value, and its metadata are stored in this chunk.

4.3 Design: Memory Management Structure for Hybrid Main Memory

Figure 4 shows an overview of the memory management structure of the proposed mechanism. Memcached allocates memory from the main memory in the units of slabs. Normally, it manages the objects of various data sizes by the slab class for DRAM and the chunk in it. In this study, we consider a new slab class for the NVM designed in addition to the slab class for the DRAM (Fig. 4, Right). In the slab structure, we created one for the NVM, the chunk size of each slab class is the same as that of the DRAM.

The reason for preparing a slab class group for each memory device is that, in addition to trying to expand the memory capacity using NVM without greatly changing

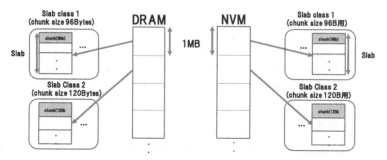

Fig. 4. Dual-LRU: extension of KVS slab class

the existing Memcached mechanism, the cache request volume from the client aimed to operate the same as Memcached when the memory size is less than DRAM.

4.4 Memcached Segment LRU Algorithm

If the Memcached server runs out of memory when adding a new item, it deletes the old item using the segment LRU algorithm regardless of its validity period and adds the new item. To achieve this, and to make general LRUs work more efficiently with Memcached, it offers LRUs with three groups (Fig. 5).

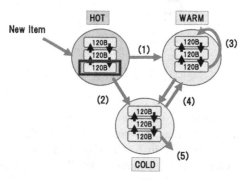

Fig. 5. Example: slab class two (for 120 bytes chunk size)

Each slab class has an LRU that controls the reference frequency of items, and the LRU is divided into three segments class: HOT, WARM, and COLD. Each item has a flag that varies depending on the number of accesses and moves between the three segments depending on the state of the flag. A dedicated background thread that manages LRU repeatedly checks the last item of the list in each group. When checking, the process is distinguished by accessing the item more than once and less than twice. In the Fig. 5, items that are requested to be saved by the client first enter the HOT group and move to WARM if accessed more than once (1), and to the COLD if less (2). If a WARM item is accessed more than once, it will transition to WARM as it is (3), and if less than twice, it will transition to COLD (4). As a result, items that are relatively inaccessible gather at COLD. The items with continuous access exist in HOT, WARM. When the memory is full, the last item of COLD that can be judged as least used is deleted (5).

4.5 Dual-LRU: Extension of Segment LRU Algorithm

In addition to the existing DRAM segment LRU, we design and implement a new DCPM segment LRU. We add a queue named MOVE queue for adding the items that have been moved between memory devices and a background thread (migrator thread) for moving items. The thread added the items to the MOVE queue between the two types of the memory devices (Fig. 6). By creating a MOVE queue, items can be moved between memory devices asynchronously without interfering with the processing of the existing LRU's three segments.

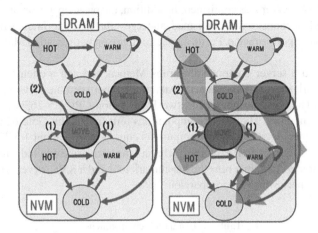

Fig. 6. MOVE queue within segment Dual-LRU (left), way of moving the classes (right).

Both the segment LRUs were connected by the two MOVE queues, and a MOVE queue for moving items from DRAM to DCPM and a MOVE queue for moving items from DCPM to DRAM were created. To check the end of each segment LRU, the LRU maintenance threads were also provided for the DRAM and the DCPM, respectively. This design was designed by considering the process that would affect the server performance itself, which is a large number of items moved by a single thread.

A new function has been added to limit the time that can be stored in the DRAM so that items with low access exist long in the DRAM and do not waste memory. If the last item in the DRAM COLD queue exceeds the set time, save the item to NVM. Once moved to the MOVE queue, it is moved to NVM. The reason for creating the MOVE queue is that if items are moved from memory to memory while scanning the COLD queue in the LRU maintenance thread, the time for which the COLD queue of the DRAM is locked becomes longer. In Memcached, if an item cannot be secured at the time of the SET command, the deletion target is found from the COLD queue. If the LRU maintenance thread locks the COLD queue frequently, the throughput drops significantly at the time of the SET command. Therefore, we consider that the lock frequency of the COLD queue was not increased by adopting the method of moving items to the MOVE queue once.

We developed the proposed Dual-LRU mechanism as a prototype for Memcached ver1.5.16. In this study, we used Device Dax mode provided by Linux NVDIMM driver. It can be operated safely from the user space through Device Dax device files (such as/dev/dax). The proposed mechanism uses mmap () to map the device file to the virtual address space for NVM and reads and writes it like a normal DRAM.

5 Evaluation

5.1 Evaluation Method

The effect of the combination of memory devices installed on the server on the performance of the KVS server was confirmed. In addition, the basic operation of the prototype of the proposed mechanism was confirmed, and an evaluation experiment was performed to clarify the basic performance. Performance comparison with existing Memcached was performed.

We prepared a server computer that runs Memcached and a client computer that runs a benchmark tool for Memcached. Data transfer between the server and the client used 10 GbE. The client computer has two Intel Xenon CPU E5-2630 2.20 GHz and 120 GBytes of memory. The server computer has four Intel Xeon Gold 6230 2.10 GHz and 180 GB of memory. The server computer is equipped with about 1.5 TB of Optane DCPM (Table 1). We prepared a micro benchmark tool that was executed with Memaslap [15]. We prepared a client that runs the benchmark tool and a KVS server. The following experiment was performed for comparison:

Table 1. Evaluation environment

	Specification
M/B	Supermicro SYS-6029U-TR4 (BIOS ver3.1)
CPU	Intel Xeon Gold 6230 2.10 GHz × 2
DRAM	DDR4× 12
DCPM	Intel® Optane DC Persistent Memory 128 GB× 12
OS	Fedora 30

(1) DRAM-ONLY: Existing Memcached server using 32 GB of DRAM.
(2) DCPM-ONLY: A server that expands DCPM 32 GB with the proposed memory management structure.
(3) EXTSTORE: Existing Memcached server using 4 GB of DRAM. The storage use function (Extstore) of the existing Memcached server uses SSD 28 GB.
(4) EXTNVM: Memcached server based on the proposed mechanism using 4 GB of DRAM and 28 GB of DCPM. Dynamic item movement is effective. Proposal server that moves between DCPM and DRAM according to access frequency.

(5) EXTNVM-NOMIG: Memcached server based on the proposed mechanism using 4 GB of DRAM and 28 GB of DCPM. Although the proposed mechanism is used, dynamic item movement from DCPM to DRAM is invalid for comparison. EXTNVM-NOMIG uses DRAM memory first and saves data to DCPM when the DRAM memory becomes full.

As a setting of the memaslap, we prepared the data with a key size of 64 B and a value size of 1 KB that were stored on a total of 30 GB of server. There were 256 connections from the client to the server at the same time. An evaluation experiment was performed with a workload that executes the Read command 20 million times. To evaluate the basic performance of the KVS server for each memory device, read-only was used as it was an extremely heavy workload.

5.2 Basic Comparison Result

(1) Comparison of existing method (Extstore) and proposed method

The comparison results are shown in Fig. 4. EXTSTORE used DCPM as a block device. The average latency was 311us for EXTNVM-NOMIG and 462us for EXT-STORE. The peak value in the latency distribution of EXTNVM-NOMIG was 290–299 us, and the peak value in the latency distribution of EXTSTORE was 470–479 us. Extstore is designed to take into account the low access speed of flash storage, which performs buffering when reading and writing, and is set to make the OS recognize DCPM as a block device, so it cannot exhibit the original access speed of DCPM. This led to the difference in performance between the proposed method and the existing method.

(2) Comparison by Memory Device

For the result of the DRAM-ONLY, DCPM-ONLY, and EXTNVM-NOMIG, the average latency was 295 us for DRAM-ONLY, 324 us for DCPM-ONLY, and 311 us for EXTNVM-NOMIG. The peak values in the latency distribution were 250–259 us for DRAM-ONLY, 310–319 us for DCPM-ONLY, and 290–299 us for EXTNVMM-NOMIG. Judging from the average value of latency and the peak value of the latency distribution, the difference in the access speed of the memory device, that is, the fact that the access speed is DRAM < DCPM, is reflected in the average value of the latency and the peak value of the latency distribution.

(3) Comparison of the proposed method with and without movement between memory devices

When we compared the proposed method with and without movement between memory devices, there are two types: one that simply extends the KVS server using DCPM, and one that expands with DCPM and moves items between DRAM and DCPM. Figure 7 shows the comparison results. The average latency was 300 μs for EXTNVMM with items moving between memory devices and 311 μs for EXTNVM-NOMIG without items moving between memory devices. The result shows that the peak performance of the proposed method was slightly inferior to that of DRAM, however, improved by 40% over the existing implementation EXTSTORE.

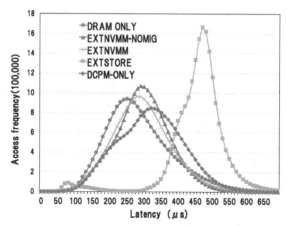

Fig. 7. Result of the comparison for the DRAM-only, DCPM-only, Ext with our proposed functions

5.3 Edge Computing Evaluation

In order to show the usefulness of the extended KVS server in the edge computing environment, a virtual edge and cloud were prepared and should be evaluated as an experimental environment. As we described in the section one Fig. 2, the most of the data were stored in the cloud, and some of the data was cached at the edge server. In this experiment, we set the total data, which was 50 GB, and the KVS server at the edge was tested on two types of servers: a server using 4 GB of DRAM and a server with an expanded memory size using 4 GB of DRAM and 16 GB of DCPM.

In this experiment, first, the client accesses the edge KVS server. If the data is not cached on the edge server, they access the cloud server. The client measures the latency until data can be acquired. Considering the physical distance, the cloud uses netem (Network Emulation), a Linux tc (traffic control) function, to generate one ms packet delay between the client and the cloud. The left block is the access to the edge, and the right block is the access to the cloud. There are two mountains on the edge and on the cloud side, but I think this is due to the small number of worker threads that handle connections from the server client. The result shows that the number of hits at the edge was increased about five times by extending the edge with DCPM. Figure 8 shows the result of comparison from the viewpoint of throughput. By extending the edge with DCPM, the server expanded by DCPM improved the throughput by about 19% compared to the server without expansion. From this result, the expansion of the edge server improved the overall latency and throughput.

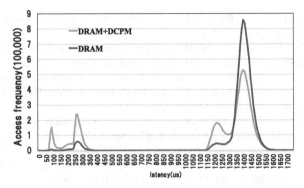

Fig. 8. Edge extension results with DRAM and DCPM

6   Conclusion

By moving frequently accessed items to a faster DRAM, access to the DRAM was increased, and as a result, the average value of latency and the distribution of latency were improved compared to the case without movement. A read-only workload was used. DRAM-only, DCPM-only, and Extstore each had a lower KVS server performance than the Read-Only workload results. DCPM has a write speed of about 300 ns and is about 5 times slower than DRAM. There was also a difference in reading from DRAM, but the difference in writing speed was even greater. By expanding the KVS server using DCPM for the edge, the number of items that can be cached on the edge increased, and the hit rate improved. In addition, the number of accesses to the cloud was reduced by improving the hit ratio at the edge, and the throughput was also improved. From these facts, extending the KVS server using DCPM has contributed to the data cache part of edge computing.

Acknowledgments. This research was supported by the Japan Science and Technology Agency (JST), CREST, JPMJCR19K1. It was also supported by JSPS Kakenhi Grant 19H01108.

References

1. Bilal, K., Khalid, O., Erbad, A., Khan, S.U.: Potentials, trends, and prospects in edge technologies: fog, cloudlet, mobile edge, and micro data centers. Comput. Netw. **130**, 94–120 (2018)
2. International roadmap for device and systems 2018 edition. https://irds.ieee.org/editions/2018
3. Intel® Optane™ DC Persistent · Memory. https://www.intel.co.jp/content/www/jp/ja/architecture-and-technology/optane-dc-persistent-memory.html. Accessed 7 Nov 2019
4. Izraelevitz, J., et al.: Basic performance measurements of the intel optane DC persistent memory module (2019)
5. dormando. Memcached wiki (2019). https://github.com/memcached/memcached/wiki
6. Extstore in the cloud. https://memcached.org. Accessed 7 Nov 2019
7. Xia, F., Jiang, D., Xiong, J., Sun, N.: HiKV: a hybrid index key-value store for DRAM-NVM memory systems. In: USENIX ATC 2017, Proceedings of the 2017 USENIX Conference on Usenix Annual Technical Conference, pp. 349–362 (2017)

8. Liu, H., Huang, L., Zhu, Y., Shen, Y.: LibreKV: a persistent in-memory key-value store. IEEE Trans. Emerg. Top. Comput. **PP**(99), 1 (2017)

9. Wu, X., et al.: NVMcached: an NVM-based key-value cache. In: Proceedings of the ACM SIGOPS Asia-Pacific Workshop on Systems, August 2016, pp. 1–7 (2016)

10. Jin, H., Li, Z., Liu, H., Liao, X., Zhang, Y.: Hotspot-aware hybrid memory management for in-memory key-value stores. IEEE Trans. Parallel Distrib. Syst. **31**(4), 779–792 (2020). https://doi.org/10.1109/tpds.2019.2945315

11. Zhou, Y., Philbin, J., Li, K.: The multi-queue replacement algorithm for second level buffer caches. In: Proceedings of the USENIX Annual Technical Conference, June 2001, pp. 91–104 (2001)

12. Corbato, F., Merwin-Daggett, M., Dealey, R.: An experimental time-sharing system. In: Proceedings of the 1962 Spring Joint Computer Conference (1962)

13. EVCache. https://github.com/Netflix/EVCache. Accessed 13 Jan 2020

14. Wu, K., Ren, J., Li, D.: Runtime data management on non-volatile memory-based heterogeneous memory for task-parallel programs. In: Proceedings of the International Conference for High Performance Computing, Networking, Storage, and Analysis, November 2018, pp. 31:1–31:13 (2018)

15. Memaslap. http://docs.libmemcached.org/bin/memaslap.html. 18 December 2019

Small, Accurate, and Fast Re-ID
on the Edge: The SAFR Approach

Abhijit Suprem[1(⊠)], Calton Pu[1], and Joao Eduardo Ferreira[2]

[1] School of Computer Science, Georgia Institute of Technology, Atlanta, USA
asuprem@gatech.edu
[2] Department of Mathematics and Statistics, University of Sao Paulo, Sao Paulo,
Brazil

Abstract. We propose a Small, Accurate, and Fast Re-ID (SAFR) design
for flexible vehicle re-id under a variety of compute environments such as
cloud, mobile, edge, or embedded devices by only changing the re-id model
backbone. Through best-fit design choices, feature extraction, training
tricks, global attention, and local attention, we create a re-id model
design that optimizes multi-dimensionally along model size, speed, &
accuracy for deployment under various memory and compute constraints.
We present several variations of our flexible SAFR model: SAFR-Large
for cloud-type environments with large compute resources, SAFR-Small
for mobile devices with some compute constraints, and SAFR-Micro for
edge devices with severe memory & compute constraints.

SAFR-Large delivers state-of-the-art results with mAP 81.34 on
the VeRi-776 vehicle re-id dataset (15% better than related work).
SAFR-Small trades a 5.2% drop in performance (mAP 77.14 on VeRi-
776) for over 60% model compression and 150% speedup. SAFR-Micro,
at only 6 MB and 130 MFLOPS, trades 6.8% drop in accuracy (mAP
75.80 on VeRi-776) for 95% compression and 33x speedup compared to
SAFR-Large.

1 Introduction

Increasing numbers of traffic camera networks in the wild have coincided with
growing attention towards the traffic management problem, where the goal is to
improve vehicle detection and recognition for better traffic safety and emergency
response. Several works in the past decade have focused on this problem [1,2]. An
important consideration is small and fast models for edge and mobile deployment
on cameras to reduce bandwidth costs and distribute processing from cloud to
edge [1]. The primary challenge remains vehicle re-id where the same vehicle
must be identified across multiple cameras [3].

Vehicle Re-ID. There have been several recent works towards accurate vehicle
re-id [4–8]. Vehicle re-id has two primary challenges: (i) inter-class similarity,
where two different vehicles appear similar due to assembly-line manufacturing,
and (ii) intra-class variability, where the same vehicle looks different due to
different camera orientations. Re-id relies on representational learning, where a

© Springer Nature Switzerland AG 2020
A. Katangur et al. (Eds.): EDGE 2020, LNCS 12407, pp. 63–77, 2020.
https://doi.org/10.1007/978-3-030-59824-2_5

model learns to track vehicles by learning fine-grained attributes such as decals or emblem. End-to-end re-id models using automatic feature extraction for re-id are common; these approaches are designed for offline re-id since due to their complexity, size, and compute cost, they are suitable only for cloud environments with more compute resources.

Multi-dimensional Models. For vehicle re-id in video data from traffic monitoring cameras, there is an opportunity for flexible and scalable models running on the cloud, edge, or mobile devices, depending on varied performance (e.g., real-time) or resource requirements [9]: edge re-id can be used for local tracking, mobile re-id can be used for validating edge re-id results, and cloud re-id can be used for sophisticated and complex vehicle re-id models. Theoretically, different models could be used in different system tiers, but it would be expensive to develop and maintain those disparate models, and their non-trivial interactions may degrade system performance. In this paper, we propose the Small, Accurate, and Fast Re-id (SAFR) approach, capable of generating classification models with significantly different sizes and speeds (from 0.18 GFLOPS to 4 GFLOPS), while preserving model accuracy (with less than 10% loss from the largest to smallest of models). The SAFR approach to vehicle re-id enables flexible and effective resource management from cloud to edge, without requiring major changes or integration of different models, simplifying deployability and improving monitoring efficiency [10].

The SAFR Approach. In this paper, we propose SAFR - a small, accurate, and fast re-id design that achieves state-of-the-art performance on vehicle re-id across a variety of datasets. Since vehicle re-id requires identifying fine-grained local attributes of vehicles across camera orientations, we develop an unsupervised parts-based local features extractor to detect vehicle parts across orientations. By learning fine-grained variances between vehicles, e.g. headlights, decals, emblem, SAFR's local attention modules for local feature extraction addresses the intra-class variability problem. Simultaneously, SAFR uses a global attention module to ensure that models do not overfit on fine-grained features, thereby retaining important contextual information. SAFR performs rich feature extraction on a single backbone compared to multi-branch networks with expensive fully connected layers covered in Sect. 3, allowing re-id models based on SAFR's design to be both smaller and faster.

Contributions. First, we present SAFR, a small, accurate, and fast multi-dimensional model design approach for vehicle re-id that integrates global attention, local attention, ground-up backbone design, and training tricks to deliver state-of-the-art accuracy at significantly reduced model size and orders of magnitude faster speed. Second, we develop several variations on SAFR to illustrate the flexibility of the approach and the robustness of SAFR models across the spectrum of model sizes. Illustrating large-size models, SAFR-Large has best accuracy for traditional offline re-id with mAP 81.34 on VeRi-776; in the middle range, SAFR-Medium and SAFR-Small achieve accuracy within 2–5% of SAFR-Large, and are between 30–60% smaller; at the small-size end of spectrum (6 MB, 5% of SAFR-Large), SAFR-Micro achieves accuracy within 6.8% of SAFR-Large, running at about 34 times faster (130 MFLOPS).

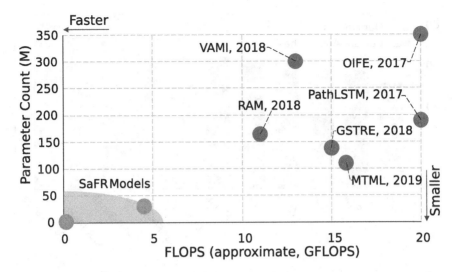

Fig. 1. Model sizes and speed The trend has been towards more efficient models. Mobile device constraints are in lower left quarter-circle, and SAFR models fit within these constraints. (References in Table 2)

2 Re-ID for the Edge

Video analytics is resource heavy yet often requires real-time analysis, necessitating research into flexible models that can be deployed on cloud and edge [1,9]. Such flexible models can be deployed in edge cameras with commodity or low-power processors and memory capacity; more importantly, they should be scalable classifiers that follow effective re-id design principles for accurate re-id (see Subsect. 3.2). Such scalable classifiers for ML on the edge can be built with multi-dimensional optimization strategies to reduce model speed and size with small tradeoffs in accuracy. Such classifiers are compressed and accelerated for mobile and edge deployment. This is "the only approach that can meet the strict real-time requirements of large-scale video analytics, which must address latency, bandwidth, and provisioning challenges" [1]. Different from model compression techniques that perform compression and acceleration on large models after training, SAFR models are naturally small and fast re-id models that achieve high accuracy; SAFR-Micro achieves better than state-of-the-art results despite being over 100x smaller and faster than related work (Table 2).

Edge and Mobile Models. Since edge models are a recent development, consensus on what constitutes an edge model is difficult. Recent advances have focused on model compression and acceleration while maintaining accuracy. Since edge models trade accuracy for small model size, more powerful re-id models are still useful for richer feature extraction. So, we develop models for cloud (SAFR-Large), mobile (SAFR-Small), and edge (SAFR-Micro).

While there are several small and fast object detection models [11,12], progress towards such edge models in vehicle re-id has been limited; approaches

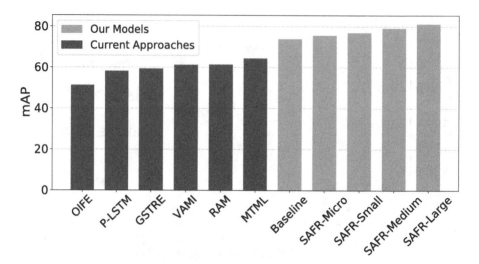

Fig. 2. Accuracy comparison Comparison of SAFR-Large and SAFR-Micro to current approaches with mAP metric on VeRi-776. Due to compression from smaller backbone, SAFR-Micro has slightly lower accuracy than SAFR-Large.

in Sect. 3 perform offline vehicle re-id without edge device memory and compute constraints. We show in Fig. 1 some recent approaches for vehicle re-id and their approximate parameter count and speed. The approaches essentially use several branches of feature extractors to get supervised features. These features are then combined with compute-expensive fully-connected layers to get re-id features. Such approaches hold limited benefit for edge or mobile devices that have low memory and compute requirements [1]. We also show SAFR models; since we use a single backbone instead of multi-branch networks, SAFR models are smaller. Our baseline, described in Subsect. 4.3, uses only convolutional layers, improving speed.

We also show trends in accuracy for re-id models in Fig. 2. Our baseline performs better than related approaches due to training tricks we describe in Sect. 4. Our SAFR-Large model achieves state-of-the-art results while being 3x smaller (Table 2) due to global and local attention. Since SAFR-Small and SAFR-Micro use smaller backbones, they have slightly lower accuracy compared to SAFR-Large; global and local attention allows both to still outperform larger and slower multi-branch re-id models.

3   Related Work

3.1   Efficient Models for the Edge

Effective model designs have been instrumental in improving the state-of-the-art in several areas [13,14]. Model acceleration has also been applied to create compressed models, including quantization, pruning, and factorization [15]. More recently, the focus has widened to include efficient model design to allow high quality networks on mobile and edge devices, such as SqueezeNet, ResNet, or GoogLeNet.

3.2 Models for Vehicle Re-ID

We now describe several recent effective model designs for vehicle re-id. Most approaches use supervised multi-branch networks to improve feature extraction. The orientation-invariant approach in [5] uses 20 key points on vehicles to extract part-based features. Vehicles are clustered on orientation to improve feature generation. Twin Siamese networks are proposed in [16]; along with contrastive loss, the approach also uses path proposals to improve vehicle track retrieval. Similar to [5], the region aware network in [4] uses 3 submodels, each focusing on a different region of a vehicle. A viewpoint aware network that focuses on different vehicle views is proposed in [6]. The approach in [17] combines four subnetworks: color image, black-and-white image, orientation, and global features. The approach in [18] proposes subnetworks for directional features in images.

There are also models that exploit re-id training to improve accuracy. Re-id training uses the triplet loss, where each iteration uses three images: the anchor, the positive, and the negative, where the anchor and positive are from the same identity, and the negative is a separate identity. The approach in [8] proposes a modification to the triplet loss to improve intra-class compactness. Similarly, [19] propose simple training tricks to improve inter-class separability and intra-class compactness. Synthetic negatives are used in [7] to improve fine-grained features.

Suitability for Edge. Since these approaches use multiple large subnetworks (usually ResNet50/152), they are not suitable for edge devices. Edge devices require small model footprints (5 M or less parameters) and may support up to 1–2 GFLOPS on models for real-time (20–50 FPS) performance (see footnote in Fig. 1) Models described above range from 5–20 GFLOPS with 50–500 M parameters (see Fig. 1).

3.3 Vehicle Re-ID Datasets

VehicleID [20] provides front and rear-view images of 13 K unique vehicle identities. With 250 vehicle models, the VehicleID dataset has high inter-class similarity. VeRi-776 [21] contains images of vehicles from multiple orientations; it has 576 identities for training and 200 identities for testing. Compared to VehicleID, VeRi-776 contains more intra-class variability. VeRi-Wild [22] is a larger version of VeRi-776 with 3000 identities in the test set. VRIC [23] contains additional adversarial conditions such as multi-scale, multi-resolution images with occlusion and blur; it has 2811 identities in the test set.

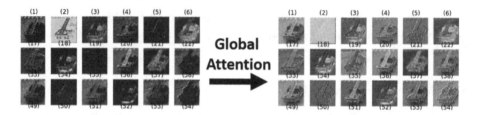

Fig. 3. Impact of Global Attention Global attention increases feature activation density. After the global attention module, more features are available to the remaining network for fine-grained feature extraction.

4   The SAFR Approach

We now describe our SAFR design for small, accurate, and fast re-id. Building models for cloud, mobile, and edge requires effective model design (Sect. 3). We build SAFR from ground up to be flexible for different compute settings.

The Re-ID Task. In the vehicle re-id problem, any image from the gallery set is ranked based on its distance to the provided query. Distance is calculated on features extracted from CNN backbones under a metric learning loss such as the triplet loss, with the following constraints: features of vehicles with the same identity should be close together regardless of orientation, and features of vehicles with different identities should be further apart even under inter-class similarity conditions (e.g. image of two different white sedans from the front view). These tasks can be classified as (i) *feature extraction* to identify the important global and local image features, and (ii) *feature interpretation* to project the global and local features to the output dimensionality for metric learning with triplet loss. Effective model design addresses both tasks in re-id to deliver accurate results. In our case, our goal is also to create efficient models for mobile and edge devices.

4.1   Feature Extraction

We improve feature extraction with global and local attention modules. Global attention allows richer feature extraction from the entire query image; the local attention identifies parts-based local features for fine-grained features.

Global Features. It is well known that the first conv[1] layer in a CNN is critical for feature extraction since it is closer to the root of the CNN tree. We found when testing the re-id backbone that many kernels in the input conv layer jave sparse activations. Also, many first-layer kernels are activated by mostly irrelevant features such as shadow. Recent work in [24,25] suggests sparsity should be low initially and increase with network depth. So, we reduce sparsity of the re-id model with a global attention module.

Our global attention module increases the number of activated features. We use two conv layers with kernel size 3 and leaky ReLU activation. The small

---

[1] convolutional.

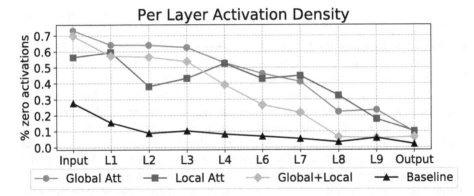

Fig. 4. Activation Density Per-layer activation density under global and local atten-tion. Activation density is calculated as fraction of non-zero activations in each layer. Each of L1–9 are residual groups between ResNet skip connections in SAFR-Large (see Subsect. 4.3)

kernel sizes increases computation efficiency. Since they reduce expressiveness and filter field of view, we use two layers of 3 × 3 kernels. The leaky ReLU activation allows negative activations, reducing loss of features. We then use sigmoid activation to generate the attention weights. Since pooling causes loss of features, we use elementwise multiplication instead of channel and spatial attention with pooling that is used in [26].

Local Features. Part-based features have shown significant promise in improv-ing re-id by helping re-id models focus on differences in relevant vehicle com-ponents such as emblem, headlights, or doors [5,7,27]. Many works on vehicle re-id use supervised local features with dedicated subnetworks to improve local feature extraction. We propose a local attention module for unsupervised local feature extraction; this allows us to extract parts-based features for re-id on the same backbone. With a ResNet backbone, SAFR passes the global features from the first layer after global attention to ResNet bottleneck blocks. At the first ResNet bottleneck block, we use local attention to take advantage of larger spa-tial size compared to smaller spatial size as deeper bottlenecks. We apply dense block attention (DBAM) derived from CBAM [26] to obtain local features from global features. DBAM learns spatial attention for each kernel, instead of sin-gle spatial attention map for the entire layer. DBAM also uses no pooling layers because they cause loss of information between layers. Since relying on only local features can cause overfitting, we apply a channel mask to ensure both global (F_G) and local (F_L) features are passed to the remaining ResNet bottlenecks:

$$F_{(L+G)} = M_C \odot F_L + (1 - M_C) \odot F_G \tag{1}$$

where M_C is a learned channel mask, $M_C \in \{0,1\}^K$ and K is the number of channels for the layer where DBAM is applied. Since local attention learns part-based features through training, supervision is not necessary, reducing labeling load. We also do not need specialized part detection modules as in [5, 27], reducing model size/cost.

Impact of Attention. Global attention increases activation density in the input conv layer. We demonstrate this in Fig. 3, where we show feature activations with. We also examine the feature activation density with local attention, both global and local attention, and without any attention modules (our baseline model) in Fig. 4. The baseline model without attention begins with low density activations in the input. This is useful for situations where classes are separable [24]. Since re-id contains high inter-class similarity higher density of activations in the input is more useful to ensure fine-grained feature extraction for re-id. Adding global attention significantly increases input layer activation density, with increasing sparsity (low activation density) as depth increases. Though local attention also increases input activation density, a combination of global and local attention ensures high input activation density along with higher sparsity at increasing network depth better than just local or just global attention.

4.2 Feature Interpretation

Once we have extracted global and local features, we need to perform feature interpretation to project CNN features for triplet loss. Usually this is performed with dense layers for both representation learning and image classification tasks. We can improve our model speed by examining these approaches to build more effective designs that span cloud, mobile, and edge deployability as well as improve re-id.

Feature interpretation is usually performed with dense layers, but it can be performed by conv layers as well [28]. Approaches described in Subsect. 3.2 use dense layers for interpretation, which increase the size of the models and computation time. In SAFR, we eliminate dense layers from the backbone; instead of using dense layer output as re-id features, we use the output of the final conv layer passed through a global average pooling layer as re-id features. Since conv layers preserve image spatial attributes, they are more useful for feature interpretation [28]. Lack of dense layers allows our models to remain smaller and faster with respect to existing approaches. Using CNN features provides good results; our baseline, which adopts only these practices, remains competitive with current methods (see Fig. 2).

Data and Training Augmentation. Data augmentation has shown surprising promise in improving re-id performance. We use random erasing augmentation to improve local feature extraction. We also use the warm-up learning rate from [19] and linearly increase the learning rate at first.

Multiple Losses. Recent approaches in person re-id suggest using a combination of triplet and softmax loss. We extend this to use three losses: smoothed softmax loss, standard triplet loss, and center loss. The softmax loss helps in fine-grained feature extraction; we use smoothed softmax to reduce overfitting by decreasing classifier confidence, since the training and test set distributions are disjoint in vehicle re-id. The smoothed softmax reduces classifier confidence by smoothing the ground truth logits. We formulate the smoothed softmax loss

Table 1. SAFR-Large performance comparison to current approaches across several datasets. We outperform most approaches; Part-Model achieves 4% higher Rank-1 on VehicleID but has lower Rank-1 and mAP in VeRi-776, indicating SAFR-Large is more robust.

Approach	VeRi-776			VRIC		VeRi-Wild			VehicleID	
	mAP	Rank-1	Rank-5	Rank-1	Rank-5	mAP	Rank-1	Rank-5	Rank-1	Rank-5
MSVR [23]	49.3	88.6	-	46.6	65.6	-	-	-	-	-
OIFE [5]	51.4	68.3	89.7	24.6	51.0	-	-	-	-	-
GSTRE [8]	59.5	96.2	99.0	-	-	31.4	60.5	80.1	74.0	82.8
MLSL [29]	61.1	90.0	96.0	-	-	46.3	86.0	95.1	74.2	88.4
VAMI [6]	61.3	85.9	91.8	-	-	-	-	-	63.1	83.3
Parts-Model [27]	70.3	92.2	97.9	-	-	-	-	-	**78.4**	92.3
SAFR-Large	**81.3**	**96.9**	**99.1**	**79.1**	**94.7**	**77.9**	**92.1**	**97.4**	75.4	**93.3**

with: $L_S = \sum q_i \log p_i$, where $q_i = \mathbb{I}(y = i) - \epsilon \operatorname{sgn}(\mathbb{I}(y = i) - 0.5)$ to perform label smoothing; we let the smoothing parameter ϵ be N^{-1}.

The triplet loss L_T ensures inter-class separability by enforcing the triplet constraint $d(a, p) + \alpha \leq d(a, n)$, where a, p, n, d, and α are the anchor, positive, negative, l2 norm, and margin constraint. Finally, center loss improves intra-class compactness by storing each training identity's centroid and minimizing distance to the centroid with:

$$L_C = 0.5 \sum_{i=1}^{m} ||x_i - c_{y_i}||_2^2 \qquad (2)$$

where c is the centroid for image x_i with identity y_i. During training, centroids are learned for training identities to maximize intra-class compactness with the l2 norm. During inference, the centers are no longer used since prediction and training identities are disjoint. We combine the three losses with: $L_F = L_S + L_T + \lambda L_C$. We let $\lambda = 0.0005$ scale center loss to same magnitude as softmax/triplet losses.

Normalization. Batch normalization strategy is used in [19] to ensure the loss features are correctly projected between softmax and metric loss. Batch normalization is sensitive to the true batch size, which varies during re-id training because of the triplet loss. With hard mining, the number of hard negatives changes in each batch as the model improves. We find that layer and group normalizations are better choices, because they perform normalization across the same channel without relying on batch size. Compared to group normalization, where contiguous groups of channels are given equal weight, layer normalization gives each channel equal contribution. So, we use layer normalization.

4.3 SAFR Model Design

Baseline. Our baseline is a ResNet-50 model. We remove all dense layers for feature extraction and use the last layer of convolutional features for re-id. We

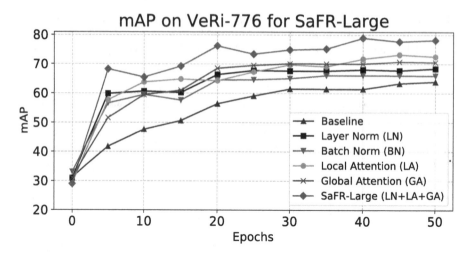

Fig. 5. SAFR Components Each of our proposed modifications improves over the baseline (ResNet-50 only). Together, global and local attention with layer norm improve accuracy in re-id.

add a global average pooling layer to ensure consistent feature dimensions for varying image sizes. During training, we use softmax and triplet loss with hard mining, with layer norm[2].

SAFR-Large. We use a ResNet-50 backbone with global and local attention modules to build SAFR-Large. Layer norm is used between triplet and softmax loss. We add center loss during training as well. The DBAM local attention module is used at all ResNet bottlenecks.

SAFR-Medium. SAFR-Medium is identical to SAFR-Large with two changes: the backbone is ResNet-34 & local attention is used at the first bottleneck.

SAFR-Small. We replace the ResNet-50 backbone with ResNet-18, with both attention modules. Local attention is applied to only the first ResNet bottleneck, since adding it to later layers decreased performance. We use center loss during training in addition to triplet and smoothed softmax loss.

SAFR-Micro. Since edge-applicable models require tiny memory footprint and low computation operations, we adopt the ShuffleNet-v2+ architecture[3] derived from [11]. We make the following modifications to ShuffleNet-v2+: (i) we remove the last SE layer to ensure each channel has equal weight for feature interpretation, (ii) we remove the final dropout layer, since sparsity is enforced by global and local attention and dense layers are not used, and (iii) we add an additional Shuffle-Xception block after local attention module to improve local feature extraction. Local attention is applied to the first ShuffleNet block after input conv layer. We add center loss during training.

---

[2] normalization.

[3] github.com/megvii-model/ShuffleNet-Series/.

Table 2. SAFR and related work on VeRi-776.

Approach	mAP	Rank-1	Number of parameters	GigaFlops
OIFE [5]	51.42	68.30	350 M	20
P-LSTM [16]	58.27	83.49	190 M	20
GSTRE [8]	59.47	96.24	138 M	15
VAMI [6]	61.32	85.92	300 M	13
RAM [4]	61.50	88.60	164 M	11
MTML [17]	64.60	92.00	110 M	16
Baseline	74.14	88.14	26 M	4
SAFR-Large	81.34	96.93	30 M	4.5
SAFR-Medium	79.34	93.34	21 M	3.8
SAFR-Small	77.14	93.14	12 M	1.8
SAFR-Micro	75.80	92.61	1.5 M	0.13

5   Results

5.1   Experimental Design

Training. For each model, we use warmup learning: given base learning rate l_r, we begin with $0.1l_r$ at epoch 0 and increase linearly to l_r by epoch 10. During training, we use a batch size of 72 with 18 unique ids per batch and image size 350×350 (SAFR-Micro uses 224×224).

Metrics. For SAFR evaluation, we use the standard mAP and rank-1 metrics. Distances are measured pairwise between gallery and query image embeddings matrices. We adopt the evaluation methods described in [20, 21].

5.2   SAFR Component Analysis

We examine impact of layer norm, batch norm, global attention, and local attention in Fig. 5. Layer norm improves performance by ensuring losses are correctly backpropagated. Since triplet loss maximizes the inter-class L2 norm and softmax maximizes the inter-class cosine angle, we need to project the triplet loss around the unit hypersphere to ensure it can be added directly to the softmax loss [19]. Normalization performs this projection [19]; layer norm outperforms batch norm since it does not reply on batch size, which changes during training (see Subsect. 4.2). Global and local attention also improve performance; with increased information density (Fig. 4), SAFR models have improved feature extraction. Local attention improves feature richness by ensuring fine-grained, parts-based features are detected. Also, our local attention module automatically detects these part-based features; this increases robustness (mAP) by reducing overfitting to supervised parts-based features as in [5].

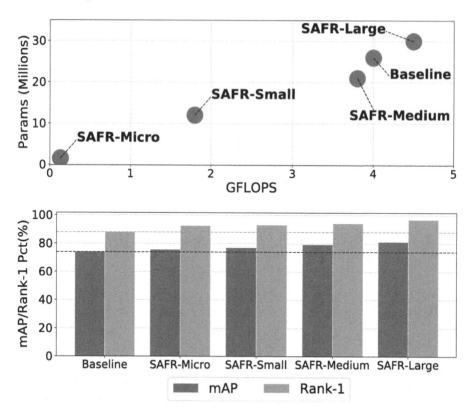

Fig. 6. SAFR Models Size (in millions of parameters), speed (GFLOPS), and accuracies (mAP and Rank-1) of each of our proposed models.

5.3   SAFR Model Performance

SAFR-Large. We evaluate SAFR-Large on VeRi-776, VRIC, VeRi-Wild, and VehicleID, shown in Table 1. On VeRi-776, SAFR-Large achieves state-of-the-art results with mAP 81.34 and Rank-1 of 96.93. On VRIC, SAFR-Large can handle the multi-scale, multi-resolution vehicle images. On the more recent VeRi-Wild, SAFR-Large also achieves good results, with nearly 7% better Rank-1 accuracy. On VehicleID (high inter-class similarity), SAFR-Large is second to [27]; since [27] uses explicit vehicle parts for re-id, it is more suited to VehicleID. Because SAFR-Large uses unsupervised local feature extraction, it has more robust performance in multi-orientation settings of VeRi-776/Wild and VRIC.

SAFR Variations. We compare our four models plus baseline to current approaches on VeRi-776 in Table 2 and Fig. 6. The baseline performs well because we remove dense layers to improve feature interpretation and use softmax plus triplet loss with layer norm during training. SAFR-Large further improves performance with global and local attention modules to increase information density and improve local feature extraction, respectively. Reducing the size of the backbone in SAFR-Medium trades 2.5% drop in mAP and 2.7% in Rank-1 accuracy to deliver 30% decreased model size and 18% speedup. SAFR-Small has similar accuracy tradeoffs for 60% compression and 150% speedup. For SAFR-Micro, where we use a modified ShuffleNet-v2+ backbone, we see a significant efficiency improvement. SAFR-Micro comes in at 6 MB model size and 130 M FLOPS, a 95% decrease in size and 33x increase in speed compared to SAFR-Large at a cost of 6.8% decrease in mAP and 4.5% decrease in Rank-1. These sizes are comparable to edge models in object detection and classification [11,30]. More importantly, SAFR allows the same model design at each level of compute from cloud to edge, allowing easier maintainability.

6   Conclusion

In this paper we have presented SAFR - a small-and-fast re-id model that achieves state-of-the-art results on several vehicle re-id datasets under a variety of adversarial conditions. We present three variations of SAFR: (i) SAFR-Large is designed for traditional offline vehicle re-id and delivers the best results while still being 4x faster than related work; (ii) SAFR-Small is designed for mobile devices with lower memory+compute constraints and trades a 5.2% drop in accuracy compared for over 150% increase in speed; and (iii) SAFR-Micro is designed for edge devices and offers over 95% model compression (1.5 M parameters) and 3362% speedup (130 M FLOPS) with 6.8% decrease in accuracy compared to SAFR-Large.

We have described SAFR, a small, accurate, and fast vehicle re-id model design approach that achieves state-of-the-art accuracy results on several standard vehicle re-id datasets under a variety of conditions. As concrete illustration, four variants of SAFR models are evaluated: SAFR-Large achieves mAP 81.34 on VeRi-776, while still being 4x faster than state-of-the-art; SAFR-Medium and SAFR-Small are designed for mobile devices achieve accuracy within 2–5% of SAFR-Large, at 30–60% memory size and 1.5x faster; at the smallest size, SAFR-Micro offers over 95% model compression (1.5 M parameters) and 33x speedup (130M FLOPS), achieving accuracy within 6.8% of SAFR-Large.

References

1. Ananthanarayanan, G., et al.: Real-time video analytics: the killer app for edge computing. Computer **50**(10), 58–67 (2017)
2. Wan, Y., Huang, Y., Buckles, B.: Camera calibration and vehicle tracking: highway traffic video analytics. Transp. Res. Part C Emerg. Technol. **44**, 202–213 (2014)
3. Chang, M.C., Wei, Y., Song, N., Lyu, S.: Video analytics in smart transportation for the AIC'18 challenge. In: CVPR Workshops (2018)
4. Liu, X., Zhang, S., Huang, Q., Gao, W.: Ram: a region-aware deep model for vehicle re-identification. In: IEEE International Conference on Multimedia and Expo, pp. 1–6. IEEE (2018)
5. Wang, Z., et al.: Orientation invariant feature embedding and spatial temporal regularization for vehicle re-identification. In: ICCV

6. Zhou, Y., Shao, L.: Aware attentive multi-view inference for vehicle re-ID. In: CVPR

7. Lou, Y., Bai, Y., Liu, J., Wang, S., Duan, L.Y.: Embedding adversarial learning for vehicle re-ID. IEEE Trans. Image Process. (2019)

8. Bai, Y., Lou, Y., Gao, F., Wang, S., Wu, Y., Duan, L.Y.: Group-sensitive triplet embedding for vehicle reidentification. IEEE Trans. Multimedia **20**(9), 2385–2399 (2018)

9. Jiang, J., Ananthanarayanan, G., Bodik, P., Sen, S., Stoica, I.: Chameleon: scalable adaptation of video analytics. In: ACM SIG Data Communication, pp. 253–266 (2018)

10. Chen, T., et al.: MXNet: a flexible and efficient machine learning library for heterogeneous distributed systems. arXiv:1512.01274 (2015)

11. Ma, N., Zhang, X., Zheng, H.-T., Sun, J.: ShuffleNet V2: practical guidelines for efficient CNN architecture design. In: Ferrari, V., Hebert, M., Sminchisescu, C., Weiss, Y. (eds.) Computer Vision – ECCV 2018. LNCS, vol. 11218, pp. 122–138. Springer, Cham (2018). https://doi.org/10.1007/978-3-030-01264-9_8

12. Howard, A.G., et al.: Mobilenets: efficient convolutional neural networks for mobile vision applications. arXiv:1704.04861 (2017)

13. He, K., Zhang, X., Ren, S., Sun, J.: Deep residual learning for image recognition. In: CVPR, pp. 770–778 (2016)

14. Redmon, J., Divvala, S., Girshick, R., Farhadi, A.: You only look once: unified, real-time object detection. In: CVPR (2016)

15. Cheng, Y., Wang, D., Zhou, P., Zhang, T.: Survey of model compression and acceleration for deep neural networks. arXiv:1710.09282

16. Shen, Y., Xiao, T., Li, H., Yi, S., Wang, X.: Learning DNNs for vehicle re-id with visual-spatio-temporal path proposals. In: ICCV

17. Kanaci, A., Li, M., Gong, S., Rajamanoharan, G.: Multi-task mutual learning for vehicle re-ID. In: CVPR Workshops, pp. 62–70

18. Zhu, J., et al.: Vehicle re-identification using quadruple directional deep learning features. IEEE Trans. Intell. Transp. Syst. (2019)

19. Luo, H., Gu, Y., Liao, X., Lai, S., Jiang, W.: Bag of tricks and a strong baseline for deep person re-identification. In: CVPR Workshops

20. Liu, H., Tian, Y., Yang, Y., Pang, L., Huang, T.: Deep relative distance learning: tell the difference between similar vehicles. In: CVPR, pp. 2167–2175 (2016)

21. Liu, X., Liu, W., Mei, T., Ma, H.: A deep learning-based approach to progressive vehicle re-identification for urban surveillance. In: Leibe, B., Matas, J., Sebe, N., Welling, M. (eds.) ECCV 2016. LNCS, vol. 9906, pp. 869–884. Springer, Cham (2016). https://doi.org/10.1007/978-3-319-46475-6_53

22. Lou, Y., Bai, Y., Liu, J., Wang, S., Duan, L.: VERI-wild: a large dataset and a new method for vehicle re-identification in the wild. In: CVPR

23. Kanacı, A., Zhu, X., Gong, S.: Vehicle re-identification in context. In: Brox, T., Bruhn, A., Fritz, M. (eds.) GCPR 2018. LNCS, vol. 11269, pp. 377–390. Springer, Cham (2019). https://doi.org/10.1007/978-3-030-12939-2_26

24. Gale, T., Elsen, E., Hooker, S.: The state of sparsity in deep neural networks. arXiv:1902.09574 (2019)

25. Narang, S., Elsen, E., Diamos, G., Sengupta, S.: Exploring sparsity in recurrent neural networks. arXiv:1704.05119

26. Woo, S., Park, J., Lee, J.-Y., Kweon, I.S.: CBAM: convolutional block attention module. In: Ferrari, V., Hebert, M., Sminchisescu, C., Weiss, Y. (eds.) ECCV 2018. LNCS, vol. 11211, pp. 3–19. Springer, Cham (2018). https://doi.org/10.1007/978-3-030-01234-2_1

27. He, B., Li, J., Zhao, Y., Tian, Y.: Part-regularized near-duplicate vehicle re-identification. In: CVPR, pp. 3997–4005

28. Basha, S., Dubey, S.R., Pulabaigari, V., Mukherjee, S.: Impact of fully connected layers on performance of CNNs for image classification. arXiv:1902.02771 (2019)

29. Alfasly, S., Hu, Y., Li, H., Liang, T., Jin, X., Liu, B., Zhao, Q.: Multi-label-based similarity learning for vehicle re-identification. IEEE Access **7**, 162605–162616 (2019)

30. Zhang, X., Zhou, X., Lin, M., Sun, J.: Shufflenet: an extremely efficient CNN for mobile devices. In: CVPR (2018)

Study on the Digital Imaging Process to Improve the Resolution of Historical Artifacts Photos

Siwoo Kim[1] and Andrew Kyung[2(✉)]

[1] RISE-CRG Group, Cresskill, NJ 07627, USA
[2] NVRHS, Demarest, NJ 07626, USA
AndrewKyung@risegr.com

Abstract. In this research, computational simulations and statistical analysis were performed with several modified mathematical functions to improve the resolution of digital images. Proposed alternative functions as new low pass filters were proved to save operation time and process. In the imaging process, when the domain of the proposed function over the frequency domain is narrow, it showed that the resolution of the final image was low due to the insufficient amount of frequency data from K-space. The main purpose of this research was to find a better low pass filter that would both improve the quality of the resolution of an image using mathematical, statistical and computational analysis. Result shows work time was decreased by a substantial amount of time to produce the final image. When the width of the function over the K space domain was narrow, low quality of image was produced due to the insufficient amount of frequency data from K-space. Higher quality of image was obtained using the proposed LPF with a certain width of domain. Also non-traditional function and its behavior of image statistics were studied in this analytic analysis.

Keywords: Frequency · K-space · Imaging process

1 Introduction

The process of transformation from a frequency domain to an image domain requires lots of operation and time because Inverse Fourier Transformation (IFT) takes every frequency point to generate the final output image. However, if a relevant function is manipulated onto the frequency space, it will save a substantial amount of work time. This study applies mathematical, statistical and computational analysis to develop a new signal process for noise removal in a digital image. Low Pass Filters (LFPs) filter out high-frequency signals and keep low-frequency signals in frequency domain. Using the MATLAB program, proposed LPFs were applied to a noise signal to examine their effect on the digital imaging process. In addition, comparisons of the functions that helped to determine the most effective filter, which was used to create a noise reduction model, has been made [1, 2].

This research performs new simulations with modified filters with a goal of determining an efficient filter that enhances digital image resolution and reduces Ringing Artifact

A. Katangur et al. (Eds.): EDGE 2020, LNCS 12407, pp. 78–83, 2020.
https://doi.org/10.1007/978-3-030-59824-2_6

Fig. 1. The process of the transformation from frequency data to image domain

[3]. Ample amounts of the frequency data are obtained from the MRI process; however, all the frequency information are not needed to determine the final image (Fig. 1).

Often, the process of transformation from frequency domain to image domain requires time because Inverse Fourier Transformation takes every frequency point to determine the final output image. However, if a proper function is multiplied to K-space, it results in reduced domains of frequency, which will be used to determine output images (Fig. 2) [4].

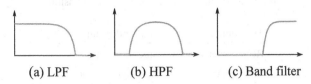

(a) LPF   (b) HPF   (c) Band filter

Fig. 2. LPF (Low Pass Filter), HPF (High Pass Filter), and Band filter that can be multiplied to the full K-space for the reduction of frequency domain

2   Materials and Methods

2.1   Filter Design

In order to produce an image domain from MRI, there is a complex computational process that requires an intensive analysis. In this paper, K-space was constructed from the MRI image of the human brain using the MATLAB software. Different proposed filters were applied on the full K-space in order to find a most efficient filter, which can be used to produce the best MRI image [1].

2.2   Filter Equations

In this study, K-space was constructed from a given non MRI image using the MATLAB software. Different filters were applied on the full K-space in order to find the most efficient filter, which can be used to produce the optimal image [1].

Filter Equations. Tested filters for the imaging process are as follows:

Trigonometric function as LPF is given:

$$k*(1 - \cos(2*pi*l/L)) \tag{1}$$

As the k and L in the Eq. (1) vary, this filter function changes the shape of the LPF. The Gaussian filter as LPF is given:

$$y = \exp(- ((l - L/2).^2)/k^n), \ k,n : integers \tag{2}$$

2.3 Fourier Transformation

The transformation from the time domain to the frequency domain (and back again) is based on the Fourier transform and its inverse, which are defined as

$$s(t) = \frac{1}{\sqrt{2\pi}} \int_{-\infty}^{\infty} S(\omega)e^{-i\omega t} d\omega$$

The FT is valid for real or complex signals, and, in general, is a complex function of ω (or f). Under these conditions, the FT defined above yields frequency behavior of a time signal at every frequency, with zero frequency resolution. Some functions and their FT are listed in Table 1.

Table 1. Some functions and their Fourier transforms

Time domain	Fourier domain
Rectangular window	Sinc function
Sinc function	Rectangular window
Gauss function	Gauss function
Constant function	Dirac Delta function

3 Results

As the exponent n in the Eq. (2) varies, this filter function changes the shape of the LPF. Different proposed filters from (a) to (d) in Fig. 3 were applied on the full K-space.

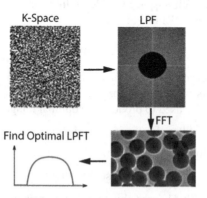

Fig. 3. Transformation from frequency domain to image domain

(a) Trigonometric function 1 (L = 2*8*M/100)

```
Filter(M/2-L/2:M/2 + L/2,i) = (0.5*(1-cos(2*pi*l/L)))
```

(b)   Trigonometric function 2 (L = 2*8*M/100)

```
Filter(M/2-L/2:M/2 + L/2,i) = (10*(1-cos(2*pi*l/L)))
```

In these two analyses above, Trigonometric function (a) and (b) are used to adjust the magnitude of amplitude over the frequency domain. And it shows that the magnitude of amplitude over the frequency domain does not affect the quality of the images (Figs. 4, 5, 6, 7).

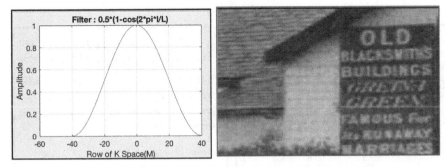

Fig. 4. Transformation from frequency domain to image domain

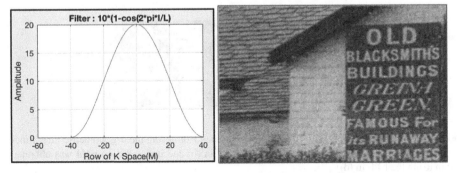

Fig. 5. Transformation from frequency domain to image domain

(c)   Trigonometric function 3 (L = 4*8*M/100)

```
Filter(M/2-L/2:M/2 + L/2,i) = (0.5*(1-cos(2*pi*l/L)))
```

(d)   Trigonometric function 4 (L = 6*8*M/100)

```
Filter(M/2-L/2:M/2 + L/2,i) = (0.5*(1-cos(2*pi*l/L)))
```

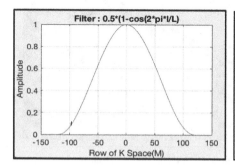
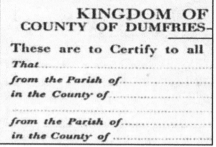

Fig. 6. Transformation from frequency domain to image domain

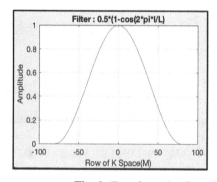
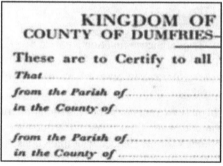

Fig. 7. Transformation from frequency domain to image domain

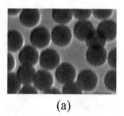
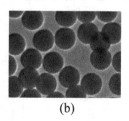

(a)   (b)

Fig. 8. Magnified bead images - Images were obtained from using the trigonometric filter functions. (Image 8-a was obtained from using the LPF in (b) and image 8-b on right was obtained from using the LPF in (d))

In these two analyses above, Trigonometric function (c) and (d) are used to adjust the size of width over the frequency domain. And it shows that the size of width over the frequency domain does affect the quality of the images (Fig. 9).

To enhance analyze contrast of the final image, histograms and histogram equalization were shown in the followings:

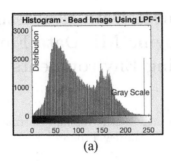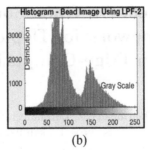

Fig. 9. Histograms to show contrast of the images in Fig. 8 (graph 9-a is from image on left in Fig. 8 and graph 9-b is from the image on right in Fig. 8)

4 Discussion and Conclusion

To produce a digital image, the data that is reduced in size from a frequency domain in a relatively large k-space that is analyzed using two different filters.

The main purpose of this research was to develop a better algorithm that would both enhance the quality of the final image and decrease the amount of time taken to produce it.

In this paper, Gaussian functions and trigonometric functions were tested to reduce ringing artifacts in every image it produced. The effect of non-Gaussian behavior of image statistics was also studied. Depending on the width of the LPF functions, the resolution of the resulting image differed. When the domain or width of the LPF function over the frequency domain was narrow, due to the insufficient amount of frequency data from K-space, it produced blurry images. Thus, when the domain of the function was wide, the resolution of the image produced improved.

In the present analysis, trigonometric functions were used by adjusting the magnitude of amplitude over the frequency domain. And it shows that the magnitude of amplitude over the frequency domain does not affect the quality of the images.

References

1. Mezrich, R.: A perspective on K-space. Radiology **195**(2), 297–315 (1995)
2. Zhuo, J., Gullapalli, R.P.: AAPM/RSNA physics tutorial for residents: MR artifacts, safety, and quality control. Radiographics **26**(1), 275–297 (2006)
3. Twieg, D.B.: The k-trajectory formulation of the NMR imaging process with applications in analysis and synthesis of imaging methods. Med. Phys. **10**(5), 610–621 (1983)
4. https://en.wikipedia.org/wiki/Magnetic_resonance_angiography
5. Stark, D.D., Bradley, W.G.: Magnetic Resonance Imaging. 3rd edn. C V Mosby, St. Louis (1999)
6. Chakravorty, P.: What is a signal? [Lecture Notes]. IEEE Signal Process. Mag. **35**(5), 175–177 (2018). https://doi.org/10.1109/msp.2018.2832195. Bibcode:2018ISPM...35..175C
7. Gonzalez, R.: Digital Image Processing. Pearson, New York (2018). ISBN 978-0-13-335672-4. OCLC 966609831

Godec: An Open-Source Data Processing Framework for Deploying ML Data Flows in Edge-Computing Environments

Ralf Meermeier[✉], Le Zhang, Francis Keith, William Hartmann,
Stavros Tsakalidis, and Andrew Tabarez

Raytheon BBN Technologies, Cambridge, MA, USA
ralf.meermeier@gmail.com, {le.zhang,francis.keith,william.hartmann,
stavros.tsakalidis,andrew.j.tabarez}@raytheon.com

Abstract. We present Godec, a C++-based framework that allows
easy transition of complex machine learning (ML) data flows to edge-
computing environments where common data processing frameworks do
not apply. Godec allows for free mixing of technologies such as Kaldi,
TensorFlow and custom modules, all wrapped into a single OS process,
making it easy to deploy inference engines on constrained environments
like Android, iOS or embedded Linux. Godec achieves this by connecting the components into an arbitrary graph specified by a simple JSON
file during startup. Despite being multithreaded, results between runs
are guaranteed identical, allowing for immediate transition from offline
experiments to deployment. The source code is released under the MIT
license https://github.com/raytheonbbn/Godec, with the authors' hop-
ing that the community will find it a useful tool to create their own
components for it, in turn enabling others to mix and merge disparate
technologies into applications of their own.

Keywords: Data processing framework · Edge computing ·
Open-source · C++

1 Introduction

While it is currently very easy to deploy complex ML dataflows in the cloud,
there are many target platforms where the environment is too constrained, or
the specific application not permitting, to make use of them. Lack of internet
access, data privacy requirements, or even just plain lack of tools (shells, background services) often prevents a whole range of interesting applications to be
deployed to those environments. Even when a deployment of an application is
achieved, it is by either restricting it to a specific framework available on the
platform (e.g. TensorFlow on Android), or a custom engine that is a monolithic
reimplementation of a certain dataflow. Often, the former approach constrains
researchers to a subset of capabilities, while the latter is usually reserved to large

© Springer Nature Switzerland AG 2020
A. Katangur et al. (Eds.): EDGE 2020, LNCS 12407, pp. 84–93, 2020.
https://doi.org/10.1007/978-3-030-59824-2_7

institutions that can afford to reimplement an entire processing pipeline for each application they want to deploy.

After retiring the aging BYBLOS [3] speech recognition framework, BBN set out to create a framework that could utilize the rapidly growing selection of available machine learning toolkits. As part of our Sage project [1,2], Godec was an attempt to create a framework which, in addition to avoiding the above pitfalls, would also satisfy the following features:

- Run on a large number of possible devices, such as smartphones (Android, iOS), SBCs (Raspberry Pi etc), laptops, as well as desktop/server environments
- Ability to easily change the processing pipeline without recompilation
- Be modular so new ML engines can be easily added (including custom modules), and importantly without having to join the various code bases
- Provide a way for experimenters to run the engine offline, while being guaranteed a) consistency between runs and b) that the live engine produces the same results
- Make maximum use of the available CPU and memory resources through multithreading, but be self-contained inside a single OS process for easy integration and minimal amount of data copying

Upon startup (as a command line executable or embedded inside an application), Godec constructs the processing pipeline as a directed graph from a JSON text file (Fig. 1 and 2), and the data is shuttled between components as messages. Godec itself has no ML capabilities; instead these capabilities are loaded as shared libraries, all of which were compiled against an API that is intentionally unintrusive, requiring little code change to existing ML libraries. Because each shared library is compiled in isolation, the usual difficulty of merging code bases does not arise anymore.

This setup allows for very streamlined deployments: a researcher can run Godec as an offline executable during experimentation, and has complete freedom over choosing the exact dataflow or ML framework used inside the graph. When it comes to deployment on the target platform, the graph JSON get packaged alongside the shared libraries and the specific model files, requiring no additional work by the application software engineer. This separation of concerns allows for quick transition of new research results, as there is no lengthy communication necessary between the two parties when a new pipeline gets deployed.

2   Features

2.1   Multithreaded, Single-Process

Each component in the graph runs independently in its own thread, leaving it to the operating system to spread the processing load to the available CPU cores. At the same time, by running in a single process, data can be directly passed around in memory without serialization or other IPC means. On CPU-starved environments this removes a major source of overhead.

```
"file_feeder":
{
  "type": "FileFeeder",
  "input_file": "data/audio_list.analist",
  "inputs": { },
  "outputs":
  {
    "output_stream": "raw_audio"
  }
},
"resample":
{
  "type": "AudioPreProcessor",
  "target_sampling_rate": "16000",
  "inputs": {
    "streamed_audio": "raw_audio"
  },
  "outputs":
  {
    "output_audio": "resampled_audio"
  }
}
```

Fig. 1. A JSON snippet specifying part of a graph. The "file_feeder" component defines an output stream "raw_audio" that the "resample" component connects to as its input

2.2   Precise, Repeatable

Despite being massively multithreaded, Godec guarantees perfect output fidelity between runs, provided the components behave agnostically to the chunk sizes they receive the data at. This condition is true for any component whose output is strictly causal, i.e. no piece of output data is influenced by future data. Strict causality however is not a necessary condition: it does for example not preclude components that take an entire speech utterance into account, e.g. a per-utterance feature normalizer, as those components simply need to buffer the entire utterance's data before they emit their result.

This feature of precision and exact repeatability allows for very strict regression tests that can check against byte-identical output, as opposed to higher-level statistics (e.g. word error rate) that can often obscure subtle bugs. It also gives peace of mind that the performance of the live engine is the same as during experiment, something that is often hard to establish otherwise since edge deployments usually lack the ability to run large regression tests on them.

2.3   Low Latency, Small Overhead

Godec is designed to process, and output, data at the earliest possible moment. If the components are written in this manner as well, this achieves minimal latency even on low-powered devices. Note however that nothing prevents a component from internally buffering its input (e.g. for across-utterance normalization). In general, the batch mode is considered a degenerate case of the general low-latency mode, in the sense that it is just a component with very high algorithmic latency[1].

2.4   Modularity

Godec exhibits modularity in several areas:

- Components are loaded through shared libraries (.so/.dll) that were compiled against the Godec API. This means one can mix and merge different technologies (e.g. Kaldi and TensorFlow) in one graph, removing the usual requirement of having one merged code base for a monolithic engine. This can for example enable third-party vendors to have their engine embedded directly into customer applications without having to expose their intellectual property. The lack of monolithic linking can also be beneficial to license considerations, which otherwise might require the disclosure of all source code.

- By providing the *Submodule* component, one can embed another JSON graph into an existing one, making that subgraph look like a single component (see Fig. 2). This way reusable "libraries" can be created (e.g. speech activity detection) that can be added to any existing graph if desired. Because each component instance is separate, Submodules can be embedded multiple time, with no cross effects (subject to the usual constraint of component code not relying on global variables).

- In order to make integration into other applications easy, there are Java and Python bindings for Godec, both for instantiating the graph from those languages (e.g. inside an Android application), or for calling Java/Python code from inside the graph via the *Java* and *Python* components, respectively. These bindings allow for a large variety of ML libraries to be used for which direct C++ linking might not be possible.

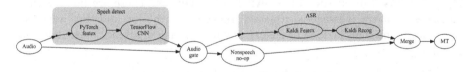

Fig. 2. An example graph that uses various ML libraries to perform speech/nonspeech detection, followed by speech recognition and machine translation. The output of the speech-detect Submodule gates the audio into speech/nonspeech. To the embedding application, only the "Audio" input and "MT" result are visible

---

[1] "Algorithmic latency" is the machine-independent latency introduced due the algorithm design (pre-buffering etc), as opposed to the machine-dependent "runtime latency" that is due to the processor performing the computation.

3   Core Design

In its basic approach, Godec is a dataflow processing framework, borrowing from ideas of Reactive Programming [4,5] and previous frameworks [6]. Each component receives messages that carry the data, and it tries to emit processed data at the earliest moment possible via output messages.

Aside from the data, each message carries an arbitrary but monotonically increasing "time stamp", a 64-bit unsigned integer, that marks the position of the message in its own local data stream.

Fig. 3. Two Godec messages in the channel between two components, with attached timestamps. Note that the apparent reverse order of the messages is due to the messages "piling up" in front of the component in the order they arrive

There are a few design decisions related to this fact:

The Timestamp Has No Predefined Meaning. The feeding component (either through the API, or using the FileFeeder) defines what the timestamp means. For an ASR engine being fed PCM data this might be audio sample count, for an MT engine it might be a text counter. The only requirement is that the smallest divisible subunits (e.g. a single audio sample) all have a different timestamp.

All Time is Local. An important design decision for Godec was to avoid some kind of "global governor". As such, the timestamps are local to the part of the graph, and it is even possible to have two separate graphs inside one Godec instance that have their own timestamps. If necessary, albeit rare, components can emit a time stream with a different meaning than what it received.

Data Equals Time, and Time Always Increases. There are no zero-time messages, as every message is expected to carry information and thus advances the timestream. This is done to ensure unique ordering of all messages along the stream.

Time Has to be Exact and Accounted For. Components need to be precise and consistent in how they output message timestamps; even a single one-off error will make the Godec network halt. Also, all time needs to be accounted for, for example an empty ASR result still needs to be emitted with the correct timestamp. These requirements might seem onerous at first glance, but in our experience they help ensure product quality and often uncover bugs.

Messages Need to be Causal. As explained in more detail in the Sage paper [1], messages can only refer to the past, not the future. This means there are no utterance-start flags (since they make a statement about the future), but instead only utterance-end ones. Nor can a message say "use this matrix from here on" but rather, "this matrix is valid up to here in the stream". This is a crucial feature of Godec and must not be violated by components, for it is exactly the prerequisite that enables the combination of low-latency, perfect repeatability and multithreading all at once.

3.1   Synchronizing, Merging & Slicing

An inherently hard aspect of dealing with multithreaded processing is data synchronization. Since the operating system is actively scheduling threads according to overall CPU load, messages from upstream components will come at unpredictable times. With a bare-bones messaging framework, it would be left up to the component writer to deal with the complexity of lining up data for processing. This type of programming, with all the pitfalls of deadlocks, race conditions, internal buffering etc, is usually unfamiliar to researchers and becomes a significant source of bugs.

Godec takes a (to the authors' knowledge) unique approach, in that it hides the asynchronous nature of the messaging to the component code; from a component's point of view the incoming data is distinctly **synchronous**. Aside from shielding the developer from the asynchronicity, this feature also means that usually only minimal code changes are required to existing codebases, since they are usually written with synchronous input in mind. As an example, this is the small amount of code necessary (simplified for clarity) to average two incoming feature streams and push the result out:

```
void Component::ProcessMessage(MessageBlock msgBlock) {
    // Retrieve the two feature streams as matrices
    Matrix feats1 = msgBlock.get<Features>("feats_1");
    Matrix feats2 = msgBlock.get<Features>("feats_2");
    // Average them
    Matrix avgFeats = (feats1+feats2)/2;
    // Push result out
    pushToOutputs(
        "avg_feats",
        FeaturesDecoderMessage::create(avgFeats)
    );
}
```

The core assumption inside Godec is that the data of each shuttled message lives on a "time grid", i.e. distinct points in time that each piece of data corresponds to. Take for example a message that contains the acoustic energies calculated from 8 kHz audio, with each energy value corresponding to 10 ms of audio. Assuming 1 timestamp value per audio sample, 10 ms corresponds to 80 timestamps:

799 719 639 559 479 399 319 239 159 79

Fig. 4. A message containing acoustic energy features at equally spaced timestamps

Now consider another message that needs to be synchronized with this acoustic energy message because they are both needed for component A, however those second features were calculated for every 30 ms (e.g. spectrum features):

Fig. 5. Two messages with differently spaced timestamps lining up before component A

Godec's synchronization code now tries to cut out the largest possible contiguous block from those messages in order to pass it into the component. This is only possible at points where **all** messages have a common grid point, so Godec will cut out at timestamp 719.

The way this synchronization is done internally is through the Godec notion that messages can be merged and sliced. Any message type inherits from the base class **DecoderMessage**, which among others requires implementation of the following functions:

```
class DecoderMessage {
    bool mergeWith(...) = 0;
    bool canSliceAt(...) = 0;
    bool sliceOut(...) = 0;
}
```

These functions are called by the Godec framework for each message during its attempt to slice out a block. If there is no way of slicing, Godec waits until more data arrives, in the expectation that it will be possible later. This is also why Godec will halt if a component sends incorrect output timestamps; the downstream component will not be able to find a common slice point for its incoming streams and wait indefinitely.

4   Analysis and Debugging

Any framework that employs multithreading and asynchronous messaging is usually hard to analyze because the OS scheduler will thwart any attempt of repeatable runs. The more complex the network of interacting components is, the more the issue is exacerbated. As an example, a still relatively straightforward graph as in Fig. 2 already has 9 interacting components: messages arrive at components at seemingly random times, and the usual debugging tools (gdb etc) quickly become unwieldy because of the inherently moving parts. Ideally,

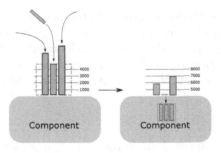

Fig. 6. Messages to each component input get lined up, according to their timestamps. A contiguous chunk gets sliced out and passed into the component code

one would like to treat an offending component in isolation, stepping through only its code and not have to rely on running other components for their input.

Godec allows exactly this. Because a message can have arbitrarily many recipients, when a bug is observed in a component, one can also attach a FileWriter component to serialize the incoming messages into a file. Then, one creates a simple graph with just a FileFeeder and the offending component, and the File-Feeder replays the messages to the component. It is now a simple matter of stepping through the component code to see where it misbehaves.

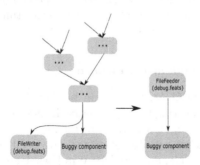

Fig. 7. Isolating a buggy component from a larger graph for debugging. The FileWriter records the component's input, which the FileFeeder plays back to the component in the isolated setting

Performance analysis of the entire graph is equally as easy. Each component can log its incoming and outgoing messages into a file via the "verbose" flag, a provided Python script can parse those logs and plots the latencies of those components. Any bottlenecks can be quickly identified this way.

4.1 Extensibility

In addition to adding arbitrary new components as shared libraries, those shared libraries can also introduce new message types that encapsulate any type of complex data structure. Godec is agnostic to the inner structure of the messages, and these new messages can coexist with other messages in the same network. The only parts of the network that need to understand (and be aware of from a code/compilation perspective) of the underlying data structures of those custom messages are the components that actually operate on them.

4.2 Performance

As can be seen in Sect. 3, the main overhead the framework introduces (as compared to a monolithic implementation of the data flow) is the merging and slicing of the messages; apart from that, due to the ubiquitous use of shared pointers and single-process design, no data copying or other processing happens.

It is nonetheless difficult to report generally applicable numbers on this merging/slicing overhead as it is heavily dependent on various factors, such as the frequency and size of incoming data, the type of messages, and the number of different message streams lining up in front of a component.

Because of this, we can only report empirical evidence from our own use of Godec in various projects, when comparing the Godec-based implementation to previous "daisy-chain of executables" implementations. So far, we have only observed equal or better performance with the Godec-based implementation. Even for an interactive audio application on a Raspberry Pi where the overall output latency had to stay below 30 ms (with audio coming in every 2 ms), this output latency was still dominated by the actual algorithmic processing, not the message merging/slicing overhead.

4.3 Platforms, Dependencies, License

Being entirely written in C++, Godec can be compiled for any platform that provides a compiler supporting C++17 syntax. Internally Godec uses the Boost [7] and the Eigen linear algebra library [8] for most of its data structures. As part of the Github continuous integration via Travis CI (https://travis-ci.org), regular releases are compiled and tested for Windows, Ubuntu, Centos 7, Android and Raspberry Pi. The source is released under the MIT license [10].

5 Conclusion

We presented Godec, a framework that at BBN's Speech and Language group is quickly becoming the standard engine for deploying our Natural Language Processing applications, and which we decided to open-source for the benefit of the community. Godec fills a hitherto unoccupied niche where complex data processing needs to run on constrained devices, while still allowing for maximum flexibility to incorporate new or existing engines and technologies. It is the authors' hope the open-source release of Godec will encourage others to write components for it as a kind of *lingua franca* for machine learning applications operating in edge-computing environments.

References

1. Hsiao, R., Meermeier, R., et al.: Sage: the new BBN speech processing platform. In: Interspeech (2016)
2. Meermeier, R., Colbath, S.: Applications of the BBN sage speech processing platform. In: Interspeech (2017)
3. Schwartz, R., Barry, C., Chow, Y.-L., Deft, A., Feng, M.-W., Kimball, O., Kubala, F., Makhoul, J., Vandegrift, J.: The BBN BYBLOS continuous speech recognition system. In: Speech and Natural Language: Proceedings of a Workshop Held at Philadelphia, Pennsylvania, 21–23 February 1989 (1989)
4. Bainomugisha, E., Carreton, A.L., Cutsem, T.V., Mostinckx, S., Meuter, W.D.: A survey on reactive programming. ACM Comput. Surv. (CSUR) 45(4), 52 (2013)
5. Java Reactive Streams. http://www.reactive-streams.org/
6. Can, D., Gibson, J., et al.: Barista: a framework for concurrent speech processing by usc-sail. In: ICASSP (2014)
7. Schling, B.: The Boost C++ Libraries. XML Press (2011)
8. Guennebaud, G., Jacob, B., et al.: Eigen v3 (2010). http://eigen.tuxfamily.org
9. Abadi, M., Agarwal, A., Barham, P., et al.: TensorFlow: large-scale machine learning on heterogeneous systems (2015). http://www.tensorflow.org
10. The MIT License. https://opensource.org/licenses/MIT

Edge Storage Solution Based on Computational Object Storage

Lijuan Zhong[(✉)]

Seagate Technology, Shakopee, MN 55379, USA
lijuan.zhong@seagate.com

Abstract. Emerging computing/storage architecture provides new opportunities and requirements for multimedia data storage, especially at the edge (close to where the data is captured). Computational storage, defined as an architecture that conducts data processing at the storage layer so as to offload host processing or reduce data movement, allows raw data to be analyzed as the data are stored. As a consequence, the data to be stored may intrinsically carry richer metadata. Meanwhile object storage is a data storage architecture that organizes data into flexible-sized data containers, named objects. Combining object and computational storage, this paper described an edge data storage platform built on a representative computational object storage with content indexed object keys. The platform provides both computing and storage scalability for Edge applications while concurrently managing the richer metadata generated in a structured way to promote future information retrieval. Using video data as a sample use case, the concept of object key design is illustrated.

Keywords: Computational storage · Object storage · Edge storage

1 Introduction

Computational storage, where the data processing and data are associated with a storage device [1], has been emerging nowadays. Computational storage moves computing closer to traditional storage devices and allows data processing in-situ at the storage layer to reduce data movement to the host CPU. It has the potential for a significant performance and infrastructure scaling advantage for applications where the demand to process growing storage workloads is outpacing traditional compute server architecture allowances. Those applications generally involve machine learning and data analytic tasks, which handle large data sets or are latency-sensitive. Processing at the application site is expected to reduce latency and make connected applications more responsive and robust. Keeping the data at the source rather than sending identifiable information to the cloud could also reduce privacy related concerns.

Meanwhile, the wide deployment of surveillance systems has generated an increase amount of video data. The continued scale-up of these surveillance systems requires streamlining the data flow from data collection, real time computing, storage, and retrieval. We see it as a promising use case for computational storage. By offloading

A. Katangur et al. (Eds.): EDGE 2020, LNCS 12407, pp. 94–102, 2020.
https://doi.org/10.1007/978-3-030-59824-2_8

the computing work to near-data or in-storage processing, it reduces data movement to remote data servers so thus to minimize the latency for real time video analysis, the core task of a surveillance system. An architecture with multiple computational storage devices also provides flexible scalability for varying computing and storage capacity requirements among users.

As near-data processing generates metadata over a large set of unstructured data locally, managing the raw data and the generated metadata in a structured way for future information retrieval has emerged as a new task. Object storage, also known as object-based storage [2, 3], is a computer data storage architecture that organizes data into flexible-sized data containers, named as objects. Each object is defined by a pair of key and value. We thus designed a content indexed object store which uses content hashed object keys encapsulated with object values to carry richer metadata. The concept is that each designated segment of a key is used to represent data source or certain aspects of the knowledge representation acquired on the data through near-data processing. The knowledge representation can involve various attributes, possibly keyword-based or content-oriented. The special designed key reuses learned knowledge representation and allows later querying on smaller sized keys instead of the data values via in-store computing. The architecture is expected to facilitate both metadata management and information retrieval efficiency on the data.

Our Contributions. The primary contribution of this work is: (i) we designed an edge storage solution using object based computational storage units. The architecture can enable or expand customer system real time analysis capability without transmitting large amounts of data to remote data centers and provide flexible scalability for both computing and storage capacity. (ii) We proposed a concurrent data indexing scheme based on object keys, which abstracts rich metadata learned in computing at the edge. By coupling the metadata with data using object as store units, we simplify the metadata management and promote data retrieval efficiency. Video data is used as use case to describe the key design concept. (iii) We built a demo edge storage platform using Seagate computational object storage hardware and benchmarked the search by key performance.

Organization. The rest of the paper is organized as follows. In Sect. 2, we summarize previous related work. In Sect. 3, we present the architecture of the proposed edge storage platform. In Sect. 4, we describe our proposed key design concept for data object indexing. In Sect. 5, we define the experimental setup and discuss the experimental results. In Sect. 6, we conclude the paper and propose possible directions for future work.

2   Related Work

While pursuing the idea of performing computations closer to data, people have named those storage devices with increased processing power and capable of executing some user defined codes as active disks or active storage [4–6]. There are studies reported on building active storage systems on object-based storage devices [7–9].

In Du's work [7], the concept of object-based storage devices and active disks were merged to create intelligent storage devices. This type of intelligent storage devices leads to the concept of active data objects which are uniquely identified and associated with a number of attributes and methods. When the procedures defined by the methods are applied to data objects, only the results, instead of the original data, need to be sent back to clients.

Runde et al. [8] presented the design and implementation of an active storage framework using object storage devices. The framework uses remote procedure calls to execute function code downloaded from client applications at object storage devices.

Xie et al. [9] proposed another active storage framework for object storage devices. In this framework, the user objects are used to store user data and the function objects are used to hold the offloaded application functions. When the function objects are executed to perform operations on user objects, the framework can partition the computation task between host and storage devices.

These systems combine the benefits of computation at storage and object storage to offload some of the application-specific computation to the storage and avoid the big data transferred to clients. However, they are not designed for Edge applications, where real time computation on large sized data near the application is desired. The real time processing generates extensive metadata, which can contain rich content information learned on the data. As interactive search on the data content is typically involved in the subsequent information retrieval, to efficiently organize both the data and the metadata has become a new challenge and called for alternative solutions.

3 Architecture

The edge data storage platform we designed targets at those applications where computing near the application is desired and large sized multimedia data is involved. The system consists of three types of functional modules: task management module, data object store module and key store module [10].

The task management module is served by a general purpose CPU, which can be a standalone add-on unit or located in existing client system, such as a network video recorder (NVR). The main function of the task management module is to distribute the data or tasks. Each data object store module is served by a computational object storage unit. Multiple data object store modules can be included in the system based on the storage and computing scale required for the application. The key store module is also served by a computational object storage unit, which can be a dedicate unit or collocate with a data object store for certain applications. The architecture of the system supports two operation modes as shown in the Fig. 1.

When the system is operated at the real time mode (Fig. 1a), real time decision about the data is processed through application specific computing. At this mode, the task management module distributes each of the multiple data streams received to one of the available data object store modules. Each data object store module then processes the data for defined computing tasks and obtain metadata, which can include data source, features, knowledge representation learned for real time decision, as shown in the dashed callout. The metadata for each data unit is further processed to form a unique object key.

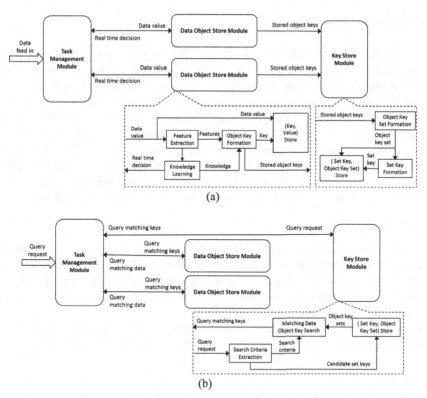

Fig. 1. Architecture of the proposed Edge Storage system with two operation modes. (a) real time mode (b) retrieval mode. The dashed callout shows detail operations within a module.

The object key is paired with a unit of raw data and stored into an (key, value) object. Those keys of stored objects are sent to the key store module, where the object keys are organized into key sets based on common segments included in data keys. A set key is determined for each set by abstracting those selected object key segments. Each key set is further stored as a set object with a set key.

When the proposed platform is operated at the retrieval mode (Fig. 1b), the task management module distributes query requests to the key store module. At the key store module, search criteria will be extracted based on the query and indexing scheme of data object keys. Common criteria are based on key words, semantic content, low and high level data features, etc. The top matching keys stored in the key store module will then be determined according to search criteria. Upon obtaining query matching keys, the task management module acquires the data value stored in data object store modules corresponding to those object keys. Owing to concurrent indexing based on rich metadata obtained in the real time analysis, information retrieval can start at searching smaller sized key instead of original sized data value. By reducing the size of the data to search and leveraging previously learned data features and knowledge representations, data information retrieval, especially at high-level, can be accelerated.

4 Design of Object Key

For content based object store, the concept is to use designated segments of each object key to index or summarize data content, which includes data source, features, sematic content or knowledge representations learned on the data during real time analysis.

For the surveillance use case with video data, when the data stream is processed at a data object module, real time analysis may be conducted to detect motion, objects, pedestrians, faces, etc. The key is designed to contain multiple segments, each of which corresponds to an aspect of metadata obtained on the original data. The key segment can be text/string based for semantic information or numeric/binary based, such as a sparse harsh code transformed from the dense feature vector learned on the raw data.

Below are a few examples of key segments for different types of metadata.

- Video source

As modern surveillance system continues to scale up, it is common to expect a system containing multiple channels, even over 100+. A bitmap index with k digits, where $2^k >=$ number of channels, is an option for the key segment to index the channel identity. Similar bitmap index may also be used to tag the data store module where the data is processed and stored.

For video data, the object value can be basic temporal units called shots. Then another segment of key can be used to reveal temporal information for each video shot.

- Video content

Popular video real-time analysis tasks for surveillance system are motion detection, face detection, face recognition, etc. The learned knowledge can then being used to categorize video content.

For motion detection, the detection result can be coded in one bit in the object key for binary outcomes. Additional segments can also be allocated for additional knowledge representation learned if desired, for example, pixel position of the detected motion.

For face detection, the detected face quantity can be coded into a binary or numerical segment. If face features are desired for data object indexing, FaceNet [11] can be used to map a detected human face to 128 dimensional vector space where images of the same person are near to each other and images from different persons are far apart. The 128d feature vector can be further mapped to a string of binary codes while preserving similarity or distance, e.g. by hashing methods [12, 13], as shown in the Fig. 2. These codes can occupy a segment in the object key and additional segments can be allocated for multiple faces. When it comes to retrieval tasks as query-by-example, face features are first extracted from the example face and top matching faces are retrieved by scanning key segments correspondent to face features. Additional temporal information included in object keys can further support temporal querying, such as, locating and tracking faces from surveillance videos.

While face searching in videos is gaining popularity, particularly for surveillance applications, retrieval of people's faces from video content remains a challenging task, due to the large volume of content present in videos and the time required to process and categorize all that information in post processing. This described object based edge

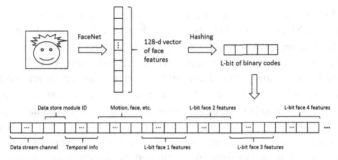

Fig. 2. Schematic drawing for generating a key segment to index face features.

video store solution can preserve previously learned knowledge representations, provide concurrent data indexing and thus promote retrieval efficiency.

As shown by these examples of object key design, the core concept is to index the object value on a group of data attributes, semantic concepts, features, etc., utilizing the metadata generated when the data is analyzed in real time. The data object keys and set object keys are stored in a hierarchical arrangement. Encapsulating richer metadata with the data value allows further information retrieval on smaller sized keys instead of the larger sized raw data. The key can also evolve to append additional segments to include more data features or contents resulting from any post analysis on the original data.

5 Experimental Results

5.1 Experimental Setup

We used Seagate Active Drive^{TM} model ST4000NK001 as the test vehicle. Its integrated Marvell® ARMADA™ 370 (1x ARMv7 Core @ 1.2 GHz) processor provides limited but conceptual near-storage computing and other characteristic parameters are listed in Table 1[14]. The maximum sizes for an object value and an object key is 1024 kB and 4 kB, respectively.

Table 1. Characteristic test device (model ST4000NK001) parameters and specifications.

Parameters	
Interface	Dual SGMII Ethernet 1 Gb/s
DR2 Cache, Multisegmented (MB)	64
RAM (MB)	512
I/O data transfer rate (MB/s max)	60
Guaranteed objects per drive	3,906,250

Through Ethernet interfaces, Seagate Active Drive^{TM} talks directly to other devices or components in the system, instead of going through intermediary devices or other compute nodes. As an object storage unit, its key/value storage interface enables clients to communicate objects to the devices, rather than blocks. Access to the drive by a client is through an application programming interface (API) and the communication is conducted by the client sending messages over a network using TCP. Each individual message is called a kinetic protocol data unit and represents an individual request or response. For example, for a message from a client to the device requesting the value associated with a particular key, the device responds with a message containing the value.

While the minimum key length is determined by the number of objects allowed in the storage space, to embed metadata in key segments, the length of the keys can grow above the minimum length. We particularly studied the search by key performance with varied key lengths. Before changing to a new key length, we cleared previously stored objects on the drive, and put 10000 dummy objects, each sized at 1 MB, using object keys with a designated length. Each key is a lexicographically ordered byte array. For each test, we sequentially requested the drive for objects with 1000 randomly ordered keys. When the key is associated with a stored object, the value of the object is obtained. When the key does not correspond to any object stored, an error message is returned. The average access times for the given object key length and access client are listed in the Table 2 below.

Table 2. Average object access time with different object key lengths

Key length (Bytes)	Access time-stored objects (seconds)	Access time-nonexistent objects (seconds)
Client: drive integrated processor		
14	0.0180	0.0036
20	0.0168	0.0037
50	0.0168	0.0037
200	0.0168	0.0039
Client: external client		
50	0.0154	0.0007
200	0.0151	0.0006

5.2 Results and Discussions

The average access time for an existing object is < 0.02 s, which include the data fetch time, and the average access time to report a non-existing object is < 0.004 s. The results suggest there is a minimal variation for the access time on the length of the object keys up to 200 bytes for a given access point/client.

For a given key length, the maximum number of keys can be stored in a key set object is determined by the maximum object value size. For a query request, the time required to acquire N matching data objects sequentially, after first identifying N matching keys by sequentially scanning M key set objects, is defined by following,

$$T = Ts + \sum_{i=1}^{M} (Tg_i + Ts_i) + \sum_{j=1}^{N} Tg_j \tag{1}$$

Ts is the time required to process the query and determine M candidate set keys. Tg_i or Tg_j is the access time for a key set object or a data object, which is relatively stable for a given access client and for a fixed object value size, as shown in Table 2. Ts_i is the time to process keys included in a key set object to locate matching object keys in the set. To reduce the time to acquire all N matching data objects, the indexing scheme of the key set store should minimize the number of key set objects to scan (defined by M) and the search algorithm should efficiently locate candidate set keys (as measured by Ts) and matching object keys in a key set (as measured by Ts_i). The design will be application specific. While more powerful in-storage computing can reduce the time for an individual processing step, implementing parallel processing can also benefit the overall query efficiency.

6 Conclusion

With rising needs of computing near the application, we proposed an Edge storage solution combining object and computational storage to scale up both computing and storage for those applications involving large sized multimedia data and sensitive to real time decision latency. While computing at Edge simultaneously generates rich metadata from learned features or knowledge representations about the data, we proposed to use content indexed object keys paired with the data to store and manage the metadata concurrently in a structured way. With such metadata management scheme, future information retrieval can start, or completely conduct, on smaller sized keys instead of the larger sized raw data and thus promote higher retrieval efficiency.

Besides boosting up integrated computing power at storage, the performance of the system will benefit from customizing object key design and generation, object key indexing scheme and key search algorithm to an individual application. These aspects will be explored in our future work along with newer generation computational object storage hardware.

Acknowledgement. The author would like to thank colleagues Bryan Wyatt, Fatih Erden and Jon Trantham for providing test hardware and valuable discussions. The work was supported by Seagate research organization.

References

1. SNIA Homepage. https://www.snia.org/education/what-is-computational-storage. Accessed 15 Jan 2020
2. Mesnier, M., Ganger, G.R., Riedel, E.: Object-based storage. IEEE Commun. Mag. **41**(8), 84–90 (2003)

3. Factor, M., Meth, K., Naor, D., Rodeh, O., Satran, J.: Object storage: the future building block for storage systems. In: 2005 IEEE International Symposium on Mass Storage Systems and Technology, Sardinia, Italy, pp. 119–123. IEEE (2005)

4. Acharya, A., Uysal, M., Saltz, J.: Active disks: programming model, algorithms and evaluation. ACM SIGOPS Oper. Syst. Rev. **32**(5), 81–91 (1998)

5. Riedel, E., Gibson, G., Faloutsos, C.: Active storage for large-scale data mining and multimedia applications. In: Proceedings of 24th Conference on Very Large Databases, New York City, NY, USA, pp. 62–73. Morgan Kaufmann (1998)

6. Lim, H., Kapoor, V., Wighe, C., Du, D. H.-C.: Active disk file system: a distributed, scalable file system. In: Proceedings of the 18th IEEE Symposium on Mass Storage Systems and Technologies, San Diego, California, USA, pp. 101–116. IEEE (2001)

7. Du, D. H.: Intelligent storage for information retrieval. In: Proceedings of the International Conference on Next Generation Web Services Practices, Seoul, Korea, pp. 7–13. IEEE (2005)

8. Runde, M. T., Stevens, W. G., Wortman, P. A., Chandy, J. A.: An active storage framework for object storage devices. In: IEEE 28th Symposium on Mass Storage Systems and Technologies (MSST), San Diego, CA, USA, pp. 1–12. IEEE (2012)

9. Xie, Y., Feng, D., Li, Y., Long, D.D.: Oasis: an active storage framework for object storage platform. Fut. Gener. Comput. Syst. **56**, 746–758 (2016)

10. US Patent pending, Application number 16/597,911, System and method for content-hashed object storage

11. Schroff, F., Kalenichenko, D., Philbin J.: FaceNet: a unified embedding for face recognition and clustering. In: Proceedings of the IEEE Computer Society Conference on Computer Vision and Pattern Recognition, Boston, MA, USA, pp. 815–823. IEEE (2015)

12. Wang, J., Shen, H.T., Song, J., Ji, J.: Hashing for similarity search: a survey. CoRR abs/1408.2927 (2014)

13. Wang, J., Zhang, T., Song, J., Sebe, N., Shen, H.T.: A survey on learning to hash. IEEE Trans. Pattern Anal. Mach. Intell. **40**(4), 769–790 (2018)

14. Seagate Homepage. https://www.seagate.com/support/enterprise-servers-storage/nearline-storage/kinetic-hdd/. Accessed 15 Jan 2020

Preserving Patients' Privacy in Medical IoT Using Blockchain

Bandar Alamri$^{(\boxtimes)}$ ⓘ, Ibrahim Tariq Javed ⓘ, and Tiziana Margaria ⓘ

Lero - The Irish Software Research Centre, University of Limerick, Limerick, Ireland
{Bandar.Alamri,Ibrahimtariq.Javed,Tiziana.Margaria}@lero.ie

Abstract. Medical IoT is a collection of devices and applications that are connected to healthcare systems via the Internet. Wearable devices and body sensors are used to track individuals' medical conditions. The collected data is processed, analyzed, and stored in the cloud platforms to provide healthcare services. The data does not only include personal information like users' identity and location but also consists of sensitive information such as mental status, drug addiction, sexual orientation, and genetics. Therefore, preserving an individual's privacy remains a huge challenge for IoT service providers. The existing techniques significantly reduce the originality of data which affects the application's efficiency. Therefore, in this paper, we propose the idea of using blockchains and smart contract to preserve privacy while obtaining data usability.

Keywords: IoT · Healthcare · Blockchain · Privacy · Security

1 Introduction

Medical Internet-of-Things (MIoT) refers to the wide range of IoT sensors, devices and applications that are specifically designed for the healthcare industry. According to the latest forecast, MIoT's worth is estimated to rise to $534.3 Billion by 2025 [1]. Remote healthcare monitoring, mobile health, tracked indigestible sensors, and remote clinical trials are few of the successful MIoT use-cases. MIoT is envisioned to improve the safety and health of the general public by monitoring and transmitting real-time data about individuals. It also allows healthcare to be provided in a distributed manner where patients and their doctors no longer need to be present in an office to monitor vital health data.

The system architecture of MIoT consists of four layers including, body area network layer, connectivity layer, data layer and service layer as shown in Fig. 1 shows. Lightweight wearables are worn and attached on individual's body to collect information about their physical conditions and health status. This data is gathered in real-time which is further transmitted, processed, analysed and stored in centralized servers. It should be noted that the data collected by the sensors may include very sensitive data such as genetics, sexual functioning, drug addictions and patient's location. Therefore, patients' privacy should be preserved in all cases. The subscribers of MIoT applications should be in control

© Springer Nature Switzerland AG 2020
A. Katangur et al. (Eds.): EDGE 2020, LNCS 12407, pp. 103–110, 2020.
https://doi.org/10.1007/978-3-030-59824-2_9

of their personal data. They should be aware of what data is being collected, where it is being stored, how it is processed and who is able to access or share it.

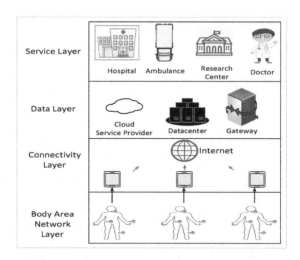

Fig. 1. Medical IoT system architecture

General Data Protection Regulation (GDPR) has introduced a penalty of $20 million over violating individuals' rights related to their personal information. Therefore, recently there is a lot of ongoing research to provide privacy protection for data collected by IoT devices. The three prominent solutions include homomorphic encryption [2], anonymization [3] and differential privacy [4]. However, these solutions introduce time delay and reduce the originality of the data. Furthermore, the existing methods have narrow application scope as they are applicable only to a specific scenario or process. Therefore, a holistic privacy preservation technique for MIot applications that has minimum processing delay and maintains data originality remains a great challenge.

Blockchain can be introduced as a digital decentralized ledger that allows users to exchange data in distributed manner [5]. Blockchain facilitates users to exchange digital transactions without relying on a third parties. It facilitates various security features, such as integrity, confidentiality, accountability, and audit-ability [6]. In this paper we have propose a novel technique to preserve privacy of MIoT data using block chains and smart contract. The model allows patients to encrypt their medical data before uploading to the cloud server. The hash of each data packet is used as the index to locate data packets from cloud server. Theses hashes are securely stored in the smart contract. Further it also facilitates patients to execute their access policy by storing them in their smart contracts.

The rest of the paper is structured as follows: Firstly, the existing privacy preservation techniques are described in Sect. 2 highlighting their limitations and drawbacks. Secondly, the importance of privacy preservation is described in Sect. 3. Thirdly, Sect. 4 presents the privacy preservation framework using blockchains and smart contracts. Lastly, we offer our conclusions and recommendations for future work in Sect. 5.

Table 1. Summarization of privacy preservation techniques

Privacy preservation	Benefits	Attacks	Limitations
Homomorphic encryption	Secure	Data/key recovery	Computational overhead
Anonymisation	Easy to implement	De-anonymization	Data utility
Differential privacy	Low complexity	Statistical inference	Data precision

2   Privacy Preservation Techniques

In this section, we present the three most widely used privacy preservation techniques available in literature, namely: encryption, anonymisation and differential privacy. Table 1 provides a summary of their benefits and limitations.

2.1   Homomorphic Encryption

Homomorphic encryption facilitates personal data sharing without worrying about data leakage [2]. This is ensured by facilitating computations to be executed directly on encrypted data. Although homomorphic techniques are considered as a powerful tool to secure and protect user privacy, these techniques are computationally very expensive as they have a very high latency rate. Homomorphic encryption usually takes 2–5 s per operation [2]. Therefore, these techniques need to improve their efficiency, before being used in IoT environments. Moreover, they are also prone to data inference attacks which involves the recovery of key used for encryption.

2.2   Anonymization

Anonymization and Pseudonmizaiton techniques are used disconnects data identifiers from data records. After applying these techniques the data such as names, gender, or identification numbers are no more related to the data subject. Different techniques such as k-anonymization, l-diversity and t-closeness [3], are used in literature for guaranteeing privacy preservation. However, these techniques have two major drawbacks. Firstly, they are vulnerable to de-anonymization attacks where data anonymization process is traced to reveal personal information. Secondly, these techniques limit the usability of the data as the anonymized data can no longer be used to derive value as compared to the original data.

2.3 Differential Privacy

Differential privacy is a computational technique based on the perturbation approach. It is implemented by adding noise to the data in order to preserve privacy.
By doing this no user can access the real data except their owners [4]. Based on
the sensitivity of their personal data the users can control the amount of noise
they want to insert into their data. However, differential privacy strategy in some
cases cause inaccuracy. Increasing the amount of noise impacts data precision.
The data distribution can be deduced using statistical inference attacks.

3 General Data Protection Regulation

Regulations and policies to protect personal data are required to protect the
sensitive and private nature of data in MIoT applications. Many countries have
started regulating data protection and privacy laws. In European Union GDPR
is the set of latest regulation on data protection and privacy [7]. The GDPR
contains provisions and requirements to protect individuals' rights related to
personal information. The organisations in breach of GDPR will have to pay
a huge penalty. The GDPR revolves around eight fundamental rights that are
given to individuals:

   i. *The right to access:* Allow users to request access to their personal data.
  ii. *The right to be forgotten:* Allow users to have their data deleted if they are
      no longer customers of the service provider.
 iii. *The right to data portability:* Allow users to move their data from one
      service provider to another.
  iv. *The right to be informed:* Allow users to remain informed about the data
      being gathered by service provider.
   v. *The right to have information corrected:* Allow users to have their data
      updated.
  vi. *The right to restrict processing:* Allow users to request that their data is
      not used for processing.
 vii. *The right to object:* Allow users to stop the processing of their data for
      direct marketing.
viii. *The right to be notified:* Allow users to be informed within 72 h if their
      personal data is breached.

According to many security surveys [6,8] conducted, there is a lack of
researches in aforementioned privacy principles covered by GDPR. In literature privacy is generally confused with security, were secure solutions are often
wrongly claimed to preserve privacy. Existing solutions mostly focus on security services such as integrity, confidentiality, authentication and access control.
Privacy is generally under looked in processes of data collection, storage and
retrieval. Therefore, there is an immediate requirement to have a effective privacy preservation solution suitable for MIoT applications.

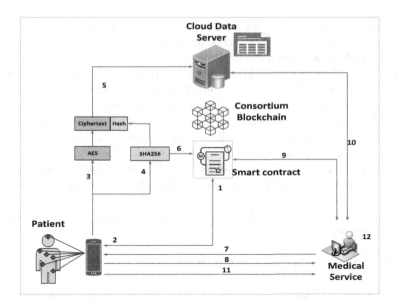

Fig. 2. Blockchain based privacy preservation model

In order to comply with the GDPR laws and regulations, a holistic privacy preservation solution is essential for MIot applications. Holistic privacy preservation covers three aspects of privacy protection including i) control over data, ii) enforcement and iii) anonymization. Control over data facilitates individual's authority over their personal data. They should be aware of what data is being collected, where it is being stored, how it is processed and who is able to access or share it. Enforcement refers to the privacy policies specified on how personal data can be processed in a secure manner by the service providers. Whereas, anonymization refers to techniques that the information is stored processed or used without being able to identify the subject.

4   A Novel Privacy Preservation Technique

In this section, we propose a novel approach to preserve privacy in MIoT applications by using blockchain. In order to implement access control policy we use smart contracts. The aim of the proposed model is to enable the exchange of data between patient and medical services in a secure and privacy enabled manner. Privacy of patient data is ensured in three ways. Firstly, the patients are provided control over their data where they can choose what type of data is collected and select the appropriate cloud service provider where they wish to store it. Secondly, they can enforce their own access control policy which allows them to decide who can access their data at particular times. Thirdly, the data being stored in the cloud is anonymized and encrypted so that the cloud provider cannot misuse or process it.

For our proposed solution we introduce five entities namely patient, medical service, data server, blockchain and smart contract. Patient is the data owner who's smart phone accumulate data from different wearables and generates data packets. Medical services on the other hand are the data consumers such as hospital, ambulance, doctor, medical practitioners and medical research center that require data from patient in order to provide their services. The data server is owned by cloud service provider which is responsible for storing data packets of patients. A consortium blockchain system is used where a multi signature scheme is applied to mine the block in the network. The block validation and consensus is controlled by a responsible trusted group. Smart contract consists of the access policy defined by the patient. The address of each smart contract is known by patient and is shared with medical services. The patient stored the hash of the data generated in the smart contract. Therefore, the smart contract have following four functions:

– *AddPolicy():* This function is called by the patient to add a new access control policy
– *UpdatePolicy():* This function allows to update the existing policy to a new policy.
– *SetHash():* This function is called by patient to upload the hash of data packets in the blockchain.
– *AccessControl():* This function is called by the medical services in order to access patients data.

The proposed model allows medical services to access patient's data from the data cloud server in an privacy enabled manner. The proposed model is shown in Fig. 2. There are total of 12 steps to be followed which are listed as follows:

1. Smart contract is published by the patient in the blockchain.
2. Contract address of the deployed smart contract is returned to the patient.
3. Data is collected from sensors and each data packet formed is encrypted.
4. Hash of each data packed is created.
5. The computed hash is attached to the corresponding encrypted data packet and uploaded to the data server.
6. The computed hash of each data packet is also uploaded to patient's smart contract.
7. Medical service request access of patient's data.
8. Patient sends the contract address.
9. Medical service calls the smart contract and gets all the hash of encrypted data as per mentioned policy.
10. Medical service uses these hashes as identifiers to get encrypted data packets from the data server of patient.
11. Patient sends the secret key to data consumer using the diffie-hellman agreement protocol.
12. Medical service decrypt the data takes the hash and compare it with the received hash from service provider.

The patient can upload access policy using smart contract function *AddPolicy()*. It can further update the policy by using *AddPolicy()* function. The patient smart phone collects data from MIoT devices and sensors. Each packet is identified as P_i where i is positive integers. Each data packet is encrypted using AES algorithm having a secret key K_p to produce cipher-text C_i. The data packet P_i is hashed using SHA 256 algorithm to form the message digest h_i. The h_i is attached to the corresponding C_i and uploaded to the cloud. The data cannot be misused as it is encrypted. Moreover it cannot be accessed by any unauthorized person as the hash of all data packets owned by the patient should be known. The mechanism also ensures Anonymization as it cannot be identified who the data packet belongs to. Only the authorized person who knows the hash can locate the data packets from data server. The H_i is also uploaded to the smart contract using the *SetHash()* function.

When the medical service provider wants to access user data it gets the smart contract address from the patient. Then it calls his/her smart contract published in the block chain using the function *AccessControl()*. According to the stated policy set by the patient the appropriate hashes of the data. These hashes can then be used by the medical service to located and extract encrypted packets from the data server. In order to decrypt the data packets the Symmetric key K_p is exchanged between patient and medical service using diffie-hellamn key exchange protocol is a safe and secure manner. Firstly it is used to decrypt the data packet then the plaintext hash is calculated and compared with the hash received from the blockchain. If they are same then it is ensured that the data is in its original form.

In our proposed solution the privacy is ensured by the following features:

- *Anonymity:* Patient generates a hash of each data packet that is used as an identifier for downloading that data packet. Therefore, anonymization is achieved as each data packet stored in the cloud remains anonymous and cannot be linked to the patient unless the hashes of each packet is known.
- *Encrypted Data:* The original data packets are encrypted and stored in the cloud server. In this way the limited storage capacity of blockchain is solved and any leakage of medical information is avoided. Symmetric encryption ensures the confidentiality whereas hashes stored ensures the integrity of data.
- *Access Control:* Patients have complete control over their data. They can publish their own access control policy in their smart contract. Only authorized medical services can get access. The data access permissions for each patients are preset in their smart contracts.
- *Tamper proof:* The hashes of data packets are reserved in a tamper-proof blockchain using smart contract, which cannot be modified. Each node has a copy of transaction record which facilitates single-point-of-failure in the network.

5 Conclusion

In this paper, we propose a novel blockchain-based privacy preservation solution for MIoT applications. The proposed mechanism allows the patients to have complete control over their own data. It further facilitates the data consumers to access patient's data without risking their privacy. The model can be used to protect individuals' rights associated with their personal data standardised by GDPR. In our proposed system, patients' data collected by IoT sensors is packetised and encrypted before uploading to the cloud data server. The hash of data packet is used as the index to extract the data packet from the data server. The indexes are stored in tamper-proof smart contact over blockchains. The smart contract also contains the access control policy defined by the patient in order to protect their data from unauthorised access. As future work, we intend to work on defining the access control policy for MIoT in smart contracts.

References

1. Market Research Report: Internet of Things (IoT) in Healthcare Market Size, Share & Trends Analysis Report By Component, By Connectivity Technology, By End Use, By Application, And Segment Forecasts, 2019–2025. Technical report (March 2019)
2. Zhou, H., Wornell, G.: Efficient homomorphic encryption on integer vectors and its applications. In: Information Theory and Applications Workshop (ITA), vol. 2014, pp. 1–9 (2014)
3. Zigomitros, A., Casino, F., Solanas, A., Patsakis, C.: A survey on privacy properties for data publishing of relational data. IEEE Access **8**, 51071–51099 (2020)
4. Hassan, M.U., Rehmani, M.H., Chen, J.: Differential privacy in blockhain technology: a futuristic approach. arXiv arXiv:1910.04316 (2020)
5. Belotti, M., Božiç, N., Pujolle, G., Secci, S.: A vademecum on blockchain technologies: when, which, and how. IEEE Commun. Surv. Tutor. **21**(4), 3796–3838 (2019)
6. Cha, S., Hsu, T., Xiang, Y., Yeh, K.: Privacy enhancing technologies in the internet of things: perspectives and challenges. IEEE IoT J. **6**(2), 2159–2187 (2019)
7. IT Governance Privacy Team: EU General Data Protection Regulation (GDPR): An Implementation and Compliance Guide - Second edition. IT Governance Publishing (2017). http://www.jstor.org/stable/j.ctt1trkk7x
8. Li, C., Palanisamy, B.: Privacy in internet of things: from principles to technologies. IEEE IoT J. **6**(1), 488–505 (2019)

Survey of Edge Computing Based on a Generalized Framework and Some Recommendation

Yiwen Sun, Bihai Zhang, and Min Luo[✉]

Georgia Institute of Technology, Atlanta, GA 30332, USA
{syiwen3,bzhang433,mluo60}@gatech.edu

Abstract. The fast adoption and success of IoT and 5G related technology, accompanied by the ever-increasing critical demand for better QoS, revolutionized the paradigm shift from centralized cloud computing to some combination of distributed edge computing and traditional cloud computing. There are substantial researches and reviews on edge computing, and several industry-specific frameworks were proposed, but general purpose frameworks that could enable speedy utilization of millions of innovated business/IT services worldwide across the entire spectrum of the current computing paradigm is not yet properly addressed. We first proposed a generalized and service-oriented edge computing framework, based on a relatively complete survey of recent publications, then we conducted an in-depth analysis of selected works from both academia and industry aimed to access the maturity, and the gaps in this arena. Finally, we summarize the challenges and opportunities in edge computing, and we hope that this paper can inspire significant future improvements.

Keywords: Edge computing · Resource management · Framework

1 Introduction

With the rapid development of IoT devices and the voluminous associated data (business, technical and operational with many real-time critical), traditional cloud computing technology could not satisfy users' requests without sacrificing QoS. Thus, edge computing came to rescue. According to IDC's prediction [1], global data will reach 180 ZB (zettabytes), and 70% of the data generated by IoT devices will be processed at the edge of network by 2025. Thus, traditional centralized cloud computing would face the problem of insufficient core network bandwidth, unacceptable delay, and more critically inefficient use of precious resources in the cloud and/or the edge. The main reason is that all data need to be uploaded to cloud servers, and the results have to be downloaded from those servers and then distributed to all interested parties.

To overcome those issues, a distributed computing concept called edge computing was proposed. Edge computing brings computation and data storage resources closer to the location where they are needed, improving response time and saving bandwidth [2]. There are some concepts similar to edge computing, such as mobile edge computing,

© Springer Nature Switzerland AG 2020
A. Katangur et al. (Eds.): EDGE 2020, LNCS 12407, pp. 111–126, 2020.
https://doi.org/10.1007/978-3-030-59824-2_10

fog computing and cloudlets. They have slight differences, while some researchers do not deliberately distinguish them in their researches. Thus, to simplify our discussion, we call all these paradigms that offload computation and storage from cloud servers to edge devices as edge computing.

Compared with cloud computing, edge computing has many advantages: (a) lower latency: data are processed at places near the users; (b) lower operation cost: the cost of running applications on edge servers is typically cheaper than on cloud servers, so operation cost is reduced by offloading tasks from cloud to edge; (c) saving backbone network bandwidth: with the help of edge servers, less amount of data are uploaded to and downloaded from the cloud; (d) better protection of privacy: since many data can be processed at private edge without being uploaded to third-party cloud, user privacy would be better preserved in edge computing.

In 2012, Cisco proposed their definition and visions of the fog computing system. Four years later, [3] presented a profound review of edge computing that proposed the applications scenarios, opportunities and challenges of edge computing. In the past several years, we have witnessed the progresses made in edge computing by both researchers in academia and global vendors in industry. Many problems have been presented, and their solutions are also proposed (at least partially).

We found that a large number of papers in edge computing have been published since 2015. When we searched "edge computing" in Google Scholar, 17400 relevant papers popped out just in 2019. Those researches proposed many different frameworks. Even though they depicted some similarities, significant differences are obvious, due to different tooling, applications, and problem scenarios. There is yet no survey paper that focuses on a more widely applicable edge computing framework. Some existing review papers usually pay more attention to specific concepts, scenarios and applications, and some easy to tackle characteristics of edge computing. Therefore, it is important to do a review on currently proposed frameworks and propose a much more generalized one to help researchers and especially practitioners to easily find out the most promising and challenging features, components and services in edge computing.

In this paper, we propose such a general edge computing framework. Key contributions of this paper are summarized as follows: i) This framework integrates most of the important features in existing edge computing frameworks, ii) It emphasizes the essential role of service in edge computing framework and clarify which features a general framework should encompass. With the help of features including job profiling, pattern analysis and resource monitoring, the utilization efficiency of resources can be maximized. iii) We also sort out the hot spots that current researches pay most attention to, summarize their research status, comment on current research works and finally point out some research opportunities.

2   Proposed Edge Computing Framework

As is shown in Fig. 1, our framework is made up of three foundation layers, including IoT devices layer, edge layer and cloud layer. In addition, we designed a northbound mediation layer lying between the cloud layer and the edge layer, and a southbound mediation layer lying between the edge layer and the IoT devices layer.

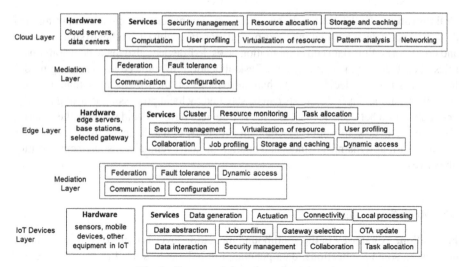

Fig. 1. Framework for edge computing.

From bottom to top, the first foundation layer is IoT devices Layer, made up of sensors, mobile devices, mobile servers and other equipment in IoT. This layer is totally distributed. In this layer, some basic features and services could be supported for devices without using a centralized controlling mechanism.

The second layer is the edge layer that consists of edge servers, base stations, and some selected gateways. This layer is the core part in our framework, including key features of edge computing such as task allocation, virtualization of resources and so on.

Between the IoT devices layer and edge layer is the southbound mediation layer, which aims to connect edge layer and the IoT devices layer and configure those services into devices in IoT devices layer.

The third foundation layer is the cloud layer, including servers, storage systems and underlying core networking infrastructure as in many cloud data centers nowadays. It does not only contain traditional features and services such as computation and storage in cloud server, but also includes some intelligent features such as pattern analysis and task allocation.

Between the edge layer and cloud layer is the northbound mediation layer. This layer aims to connect the edge and the cloud and enable their collaboration.

Next, we will explain key features in each layer.

2.1 IoT Devices Layer

Job Profiling. This feature collects "representative" sets of resource requests on when, where, and how much a specific resource wanted is generated for every considered application or application component. And it can be described as multiple resource schedulable units [49] that will be further explained later.

Collaboration. Collaboration is an important component for edge computing. IoT devices support decision-making tasks by collaborating with each other to share resource and task information, data and computation tasks. IoT devices also make decisions on the roles of each device in an IoT system. Task allocation: In some edge computing model, IoT devices need to decide how to handle requests on their own rather than a central controller in upper layer. Requests can be satisfied by local processing in a single device or collaboration between devices. So, the IoT devices have to decide on how the tasks are processed. The task allocation mechanism should be dynamic and programmable so it can meet various dynamic business and operational and eventually resource optimization objectives.

2.2 Mediation Layer

Federation. A gateway in the southbound mediation layer is connected to a set of IoT devices. In some applications, data generated in IoT devices need to be collected and transferred to the central cloud. Therefore, the gateway acts like an aggregation point, receiving data from various devices and encapsulating them in a standard way. Besides, it also needs to distribute data to heterogeneous IoT devices. A gateway in the northbound mediation layer also needs to shoulder similar responsibility.

Dynamic Access. Many IoT devices are mobile devices, indicating that any device can join or leave the edge network at any time. First, the gateway should be aware of the status that if a device is in its coverage or not. Next, the gateway should handle the user handoff between adjacent edge servers. Then the gateway should migrate the task to the current corresponding edge server. Besides, users' mobility can be predicted in some way. The gateway can combine models learned from historical data with real-time information to predict the user trajectories. The task scheduler can take these predictions into account to make better utilization of resources while minimize migration cost.

Configuration. In some application scenarios, the number of devices connected to a gateway can be tremendous. Due to limited resources, traditional naming algorithm like DNS and IP is no longer suitable in IoT environment. So, the gateway should name and index all devices in a scalable and lightweight manner.

2.3 Edge Layer

Virtualization of Resources. Given the heterogeneity of edge devices, we need a general description of all resources including CPU, memory, storage, bandwidth, energy etc. This can be accomplished by resource virtualization. There is a variety of edge devices like smart AP and micro data center with corresponding processing capabilities that makes it very hard to construct a universal framework of virtualization. Thus, before virtualization, we can use standard tests to quantify the resources of each device involved in the edge layer. Based on its normalized performance on running standard tests, each device's resources can be marked as the number of multi-resource schedulable units [49]. We will introduce details of MRSU in Selected Works on Resource Management.

Resource Monitoring. The available resources of each node are dynamic and historical data and operational statistics can be of great help in predicting future demand patterns. Therefore, to achieve real-time task allocation and make use of historical patterns, the service layer should monitor the global distribution of resources in edge devices.

Job Profiling. Every application can be partitioned into a set of jobs. Jobs belonging to one application can be described by a Directed Acyclic Graph (DAG). Each job's demand for resources can be defined (either statically or in some adaptive fashion) the number of multiples of MRSUs, as proposed in [49].

Task Allocation. When requests and data are received from IoT devices, the edge layer should determine how to deal with these requests. Demands can be satisfied by local processing in a single edge device, collaboration between edge devices and cross-layer collaboration with the Cloud. Similar to the same feature in IoT devices layer, the task allocation mechanism should be flexible and programmable to adapt to various application scenarios and operating environments. For example, some systems are battery-powered but not latency-sensitive, so these systems aim to optimize energy consumption. In contrast, vehicular network aided autonomous driving emphasizes much more on reducing latency.

2.4 Cloud Layer

Pattern Analysis. Based on historical global operation data, the cloud can use techniques such as machine learning to abstract patterns of resource demand, service provider features etc. In turn, the cloud can pre-allocate resources based on predictions.

User Profiling. As for traditional cloud computing, cloud in edge computing can provide the interfaces for users to manually define their demands and preferences.

Resource Allocation. When requests and data are received from the edge layer, the cloud has to satisfy them by allocating and activating its resources and services. The allocation algorithm could be set in many different ways to meet specific requests, and again, it should be dynamic and programmable to meet various operational and optimization goals.

Virtualization of Resources. In order to satisfy users' requests, we need a general description of all resources including CPU/GPU, memory and storage and network bandwidth, then we can lease these resources to the users with some mutual agreement.

3 Analysis of Research Works in Edge Computing

This section aims to analyze past five years of research publications from both academia and industry, based on our proposed framework. As Edge computing has experienced a rapid growth, technology giants like Microsoft, IBM, Huawei, CISCO etc. have announced and started to implement ambitious plan for investments and developments. It is time to analyze what we have achieved and what are the gaps or obstacles for successful adoption of edge computing. Besides, it is beneficial to compare the progresses and differences in the academia and the industry.

3.1   State-of-the-Art in Academia

We have reviewed about one hundred peer-reviewed research papers, and we found that although these papers focus on various fields in edge computing, several topics received much more attention. However, some important issues are ignored by most researchers.

Summary of Research Papers. We sorted all features in our framework into two categories. One contains the features in Edge layer and Cross-layer, and the other includes the features in IoT Devices layer, Cloud layer and Mediation layer. The reason why we sort features this way is that services of edge layer is the core of our framework and cross-layer features are usually a part of services in edge layer and the other layers receive relatively less attention. The total number of articles reviewed is 91, of which 35 articles focus on the features of IoT Devices layer, Cloud layer and Mediation layer. And all articles took at least one cross-layer feature or edge layer feature into account. This simply indicated that edge layer and cross-layer features were paid much more attention. It also agrees with the idea that the services of edge layer are the core.

Edge Layer and Cross-layer Features. Figure 2 shows the level of coverage for each feature.

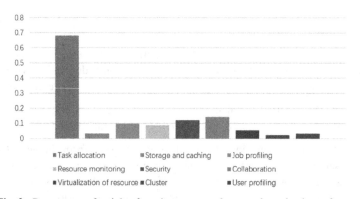

Fig. 2. Percentage of articles focusing on cross-layer and service layer features

As is depicted in Fig. 2, almost 70% of the 91 peer-reviewed articles focus on task allocation and many of them only focus on this topic. Different from cloud computing, the number of devices involved in edge computing is tremendously high and resources are usually limited, indicating that a well scalable and efficient task allocation algorithm is indispensable for edge computing. Currently, most algorithms [4–15] are based on traditional optimization theories like convex optimization and a few papers start from a multi-objective- multiple-constraints (some competing or even contradictory) decision-making perspective [14, 16–19]. But recently, researchers begin to solve this problem via machine learning that may lead to promising solution in the near future [20–23].

Some algorithms perform well under simulations specifically designed by researchers [4, 11, 16, 24–28]. But these simulations were typically not real-world scenarios and scalability may not be achievable if such algorithms were implemented in real world. Designing an efficient and universal task allocation mechanism is still a challenge.

Among the other features, security [5, 29–37] and job profiling [4, 14, 38–43] received relatively high attention. These two features are vital to edge computing. Some features, user profiling for example, may be implemented based on existing mechanisms in existing cloud computing paradigm. But in the era of edge computing, many devices are resource-constrained, i.e., these devices cannot afford traditional security mechanisms. Job profiling is fundamental for task allocation. However, many papers still use naive descriptions of tasks and the relationship among tasks or services is rarely considered or extremely simplified in their models.

IoT Layer, Mediation Layer and Cloud Layer Features. Compared to Edge layer and Cross-layer, the features in other layers are less popular. Figure 3 describes the proportion of the 35 papers focusing on each feature. More than a quarter of the papers were on dynamic access, especially all the works on vehicular networks [10, 24, 27, 44–48]. Mobility of users is a typical characteristic of edge computing. Mobility has been extensively studied in radio access network researches. So, handoff is not a challenge for edge computing. Users can move among areas covered by different edge servers before a task can be completed. In such scenarios, task migration is necessary. But migration cost is usually high. So, challenges brought by mobility in edge computing is how to keep a balance between QoS and migration cost and how to model mobility of users for merging user mobility into task allocation. Pattern analysis receives least attention. But it is of great importance to optimize system efficiency and operation cost. Because analysis of historical user demands can be used to pre-allocate resources efficiently and automatically, avoiding the labor-intensive manual allocation. And the system can then react to fluctuation of user demands more swiftly.

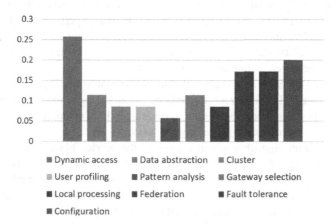

Fig. 3. Percentage of articles focusing on features in IoT layer, communication layer and cloud layer

Selected Works on Resource Management. [49] proposed the idea of multi-resource schedulable unit (MRSU) in 2015. This definition and corresponding algorithms were designed for resource management in data center networks. An MRSU is a minimum multidimensional schedulable unit for a single multi-tenant data center comprising a specified amount of computing, memory, storage, and networking resources that are jointly schedulable and serve a minimum scale application with required quality-of-service (QoS). The allocation of MRSU is fulfilled by the weighted queuing scheduling method. Compared to the traditional VM-based algorithm, MRSU achieves a lower absolute value of misallocation coefficient on average. MRSU is much less likely to under-allocate resources to tenants. From a user's perspective, the QoS is obviously improved. For both over-allocation and under-allocation cases, the average misallocation coefficient always begins to rise slower than VM algorithm as the average load rises.

[50] published a framework (ADARM) designed for application-driven and adaptive resource management of large-scale cloud data centers, which achieves resource usage maximization with minimum cost and management complexity. ADARM makes on-demand resource decisions based on patterns of the tenants' application (application profiles) rather than allocating a fixed and preset amount of resources. The historical information about resource usage is well stored in the data warehouse. The multidimensional distributed hashing table (MDDHT) is proposed to model the relationship between network paths and other dimensions like tenant, application. And it makes use of resource information from various perspectives efficient. Information stored in MDDHT can handle most requests by matching requests with historical decisions without invoking complex algorithms. Global resource allocation and optimization is fulfilled with the help of MRSU.

[26] proposed a task offloading mechanism based on game theory. The authors formulate the distributed computation offloading decision making problem among mobile device users as a multi-user computation offloading game. The optimal solution is fulfilled at the Nash equilibrium. They consider a slotted time structure for the computation offloading decision update. According to their simulation, its performance is similar to that of the centralized method, but all users do not bother to upload all of their parameters to the cloud. Network overhead is reduced, and privacy is preserved. Besides, the algorithm also converges within reasonable timeslots.

[19] proposed the Edge Mesh paradigm, aiming to enable distributed intelligence in IoT via edge devices. In this paradigm, tasks are modeled as a directed acyclic graph. The authors proposed a genetic algorithm to find the optimal solution which minimizes the total energy consumption of processing all tasks.

[27] proposed an algorithm which optimizes the service placement policy under the constraint of long-term cost budget. User's mobility asks for the migration of tasks between different edge servers. Otherwise, the latency may be unacceptably large. But the long-term budget of migration cost is limited. A balance between cost and latency should be reached. The authors assumed that the system operates in a slotted structure. Each time frame consists of T timeslots. For each timeframe, the system predicts the trajectory of users by the deep learning method of long short-term memory (LSTM). Then the problem is formulated as path planning problem solved by Dijkstra's algorithm. The weight of each edge in the graph is the service cost including communication delay and migration cost. The proposed algorithm outperforms the other benchmarking methods

in all scenarios of long-term migration cost budget. Besides, this algorithm provides a parameter for setting the importance of latency in the optimization problem.

[28] studied the data-aware task allocation problem to jointly schedule task and network flows in the collaborative edge computing. As they correctly stated, network congestion was ignored by most researches on task allocation. So, they proposed an algorithm to minimize the completion time of applications. This paper utilized a multistage greedy adjustment (MSGA) algorithm and an enhanced version of Destination Adjustment algorithm. It consists of three stages: a) Inputting the graph of task, then creating an initial schedule without considering network congestion (MSGA algorithm); b) detecting the network flow conflicts; c) resolving the network flow conflicts by adjusting both the placement of tasks and the bandwidth of the flows (Destination Adjustment algorithm). The algorithm is application-neutral, indicating that it can be suitable in different scenarios. Simulation presents that the proposed algorithm performs better on completion time of applications, but worse on running time of the task allocation algorithm. Improvement of efficiency is necessary.

[11] created a multi-objective model on IoT application placement. This model considers three objectives (completion time, energy consumption and economic cost). And it applies a genetic multi-objective optimization algorithm (NSGA-II) to solve it. After carefully setting the optimization problem, it becomes NP-complete, which means we can easily handle it by some classic algorithms. While many other papers dealing with the same problem set it as NP-hard problems. Compared to benchmarking methods, the proposed algorithm achieves much lower energy consumption and completion time with acceptable economic cost.

3.2 State-of-the-Art in Industry

In the past decade, we have witnessed the increasing popularity of cloud computing, and the development of giant companies in cloud computing market. Explosive growth of data and resource demand stimulate the commercialization of edge computing, as traditional centralized cloud computing no longer meets users' requirements. Thus, many technology giants actively join and lead in the new competition and try their best to attract adoption of their service or infrastructure. Compared to academia, these companies interact with users more directly and frequently. It is interesting to observe and compare progress made in industry and compare it with that in academia.

As is listed in Fig. 4, Google, Microsoft and Amazon are traditional cloud service providers. As world-wide leading communication infrastructure and services providers, Huawei and Cisco helped to establish and lead two edge computing alliance. According to their white papers and product introduction [51–55], we can analyze where their current or future edge computing solutions focus on. Similar to academia, all companies pay attention to features related to resource management such as task allocation and resource monitoring. As most academic research papers focus on task allocation, the solutions provided by the industry must be mature enough to be utilized, so each solution covers much more features than the pure research papers. As is stated before, pattern analysis receives least attention in academia, but three of these five companies specifically state their products' support for pattern analysis [51–53]. The industry has realized the importance of historical data and its potential power in improving both resource and management efficiency and complexity.

Technology Giants	Services/Technology Alliance	Mapping to our Framework
Google	Cloud IoT Core	security management, communication, configuration, virtualization of resource, resource monitoring, task allocation, pattern analysis
Amazon	AWS IIoT	local processing, resource monitoring, security management, virtualization of resource, task allocation, communication, configuration, collaboration, pattern analysis, fault tolerance, data abstraction, OTA update
Microsoft	Azure IoT Edge	virtualization of resource, storage and caching, job profiling, resource monitoring, task allocation, configuration,
Cisco	OpenFog	task allocation, communication, security management, configuration, data abstraction, pattern analysis, federation, resource monitoring
Huawei	Edge Computing Consortium	resource monitoring, security management, virtualization of resource, task allocation, OTA update, data interaction, communication, configuration, federation, fault tolerance, data abstraction

Fig. 4. The technology giants' involvement and products in edge computing

4   Challenges and Opportunities

In the past several years, many problems have been presented with good solutions, even though some of them might be too simplistic or only addressed part of the problems. Edge computing has not been as technically mature as cloud computing, indicating that there are still technical challenges preventing its adoption and promotion. In addition, non-technical issues like pricing strategies should also be considered. In the following sections, we summarize the current challenges that still exist and also opportunities for stakeholders.

4.1   Resource Management

Resource management has always been a crucial topic of network systems. Cloud computing has boosted the development of virtualization of resources and corresponding resource management strategies. However, compared to cloud computing, the exponential growth of Edge/IoT devices and corresponding growth of resources and data make system design much more complicated. Computing resources are no longer placed only in the central cloud servers, now they could reside in various layers of the edge computing ecosystem. As resources have been virtualized, the power of resource virtualization has not been fully exploited. Virtualized resources cannot "flow" well. In many application scenarios of cloud computing, fixed amount of resources is assigned to each tenant periodically based on manually defined policies. However, the fluctuation of each user's demand is much more frequent than the assignment of resources. As a result, the utilization efficiency of resources is low, leading to the waste of precious resources in idle time and violation of QoS in peak hours. In edge computing system, much more resources have to be managed. To make it more complex, resources in edge computing system is no longer homogeneous. Computing power is enabled by various devices with different capabilities. Besides, resources scatter in many places geologically. Therefore, migration cost of applications become another factor we should address. Additionally, devices can join and leave the edge computing system at any time. Thus, dynamic access to resources becomes another problem of resource management, and "plug and play" should be supported. In a word, how to build a general framework to manage massive amount of heterogeneous resources efficiently is one of the key challenges for edge computing.

To merge various resources and utilize them efficiently, as is stated in our framework, MRSU could be a solution [49]. Adoption of MRSU makes fast modification of resource placement policy possible. So, the controller (could be placed anywhere in the framework, centralized or distributed) can respond to the fluctuation of both demands and supplies swiftly. All the demands from IoT devices can be expressed as multiples of the MRSU. After benchmarking, every node's virtualized resources can be expressed as MRSUs and their heterogeneity in physical resources is overcome. Besides, application of Big Data/AI can be introduced into resource management. The introduction of SDN inspires people to differentiate data flows by considering more realistic criteria. Similar to this, temporal and spatial patterns of demands and resources are also the precious asset to resource management. With the help of Big Data/AI, the power of historical patterns can be utilized, i.e., pattern analysis. Based on the historical patterns, we can predict future patterns and allocate resources in advance to maximize the efficiency.

4.2   Modification of Application Model

Traditional applications run in cloud computing systems are centralized, i.e., users send their requests to the cloud and the central cloud servers process requests and send results back to users. Computation-intensive applications like deep learning applications comprise a big share of cloud computing market. Compared to cloud computing, computing power in edge computing is distributed and each device's capability is limited. Therefore, it is challenging to migrate the resource-consuming applications from cloud to edge. How to make use of the distributed nature of resources and how to overcome the limitation of resources of each device are two essential problems. Modification of application model is indispensable. To make applications suitable for edge computing system, inherent support for task distribution is necessary. Federated learning can be an example. Different from traditional centralized machine learning, datasets are not uploaded to the central cloud servers. Instead, each edge device can improve a shared model by its computing resources and local small datasets. Thus, edge devices do not need substantial resources to accomplish machine learning tasks. Edge devices do not necessarily need to upload or exchange datasets with cloud servers or other edge devices. Federated learning models are particularly designed to fit the properties of edge computing system. In this way, edge devices can also process computation-intensive machine learning tasks. Besides, local data are not shared. So, user privacy and data security are preserved better, which also encourages the promotion of machine learning in privacy-sensitive fields.

4.3 Collaboration

Different from cloud computing, edge servers are usually geologically distributed, and many service providers only operate in a small area. If an edge computing system wants more users to join, the collaboration of different service providers will be necessary. In data centers, powerful servers are internally connected, and they work as a whole. Communication cost of collaboration is relatively low because these servers are connected by wired high-speed network. But in edge computing systems, cost of communication between edge/IoT devices cannot be ignored in many cases. What is more, collaboration cannot exist without a billing system. Edge servers are run by various companies, and these servers are heterogeneous. In cloud computing, many service providers allocate a fixed amount of resources to their tenants and count how many hours the resources are used. Typically, applications run in cloud continuously for a long time. However, update of resource allocation in an efficient edge computing system will be frequent and dynamic, making the traditional billing strategy invalid. The collaboration between service providers will make the situation more complex. How to charge the tenants for renting resources is an important issue. Therefore, we need a billing system fitting the fashion in which resources are allocated.

To fulfill efficient collaboration, we need to collect the communication cost of collaboration between devices and add them to the resource management policy. In addition, charge for use should take both amount of resources and how much time they are used into consideration. Since the resources are allocated periodically and frequently, the billing system can count how many MRSUs are assigned to each user during each period. Then, the charge is based on the sum of MRSU in each period. And service providers can make an agreement on the charge for each MRSU.

4.4 Security and Privacy

Nowadays, researchers tend to focus more on performance instead of system security and user privacy. As a result, many systems have protocol-level security deficiency and sensitive data are not well protected. Current security protocols are not suitable in edge computing due to limited resources and enormous number of devices. IoT devices with limited or no processing ability like sensors and actuators cannot handle the complicated security protocols including encryption and decryption. Massive number of devices are connected to one edge device, current protocols may not be scalable in such IoT scenarios. However, regulations like EU GDPR arose more people's attention to network security and their privacy. To convince potential users to use edge computing, a systematic-level security mechanism is indispensable. To fulfill this goal, the idea of security-by-design should be widely adopted by stakeholders. Security protection should be provided by manufacturers instead of implemented by users. In addition, preventive protection is meaningful. With the help of pattern analysis, the system can detect users with abnormal actions and prevent potential attacks from these users.

4.5 Customization

Internet has become a hot topic. Many countries like China, the US, Germany and Japan has also published their national strategies on promoting industrial Internet. According to McKinsey, industrial Internet can create 11100 billion of US dollars of GDP. Industrial Internet is a big market. But in industry, many edge/IoT devices have to run in relatively extreme environments and maintenance is and expensive. In many cases, reliability is more important than performance. Robustness is highly treasured. But in general, robustness means sacrifice of performance, i.e. access to resources is limited. Currently, researchers designed their benchmark simulations that seldom take specific operation environments into account. Besides, specifically designed hardware is very common in industry and they are not compatible with each other. Communication protocols are omnifarious. Without enhancement of reliability and adaption to heterogeneity, it is hard to convince industry partners to invest in edge computing. So, collaboration with industry partners on designing edge computing systems suitable for specific environments is needed. It is also vital to quickly establish industry standards to enable fast inter-working of heterogeneous devices.

If the edge computing system is designed to be an update of the traditional cloud computing, we can add a middle mediation layer to abstract those various appliances. The upper layers communicate with the mediation layer via general protocols. And the mediation layer decapsulate the messages and convert them into specific formats. For a new system, software-defined controller is a promising choice. Hardware applied in different scenarios can be generalized and it is the software enable each controller's specific capability. Thus, cost of hardware can be reduced. Given limited resources, application and protocol developers can modify their applications to adapt to real resource limitation.

5 Conclusion

Edge computing has attracted tremendous attention from both academia and industry. Given the ever-increasing demand for resources, more critical requirement of QoS, and the exploding number of users and devices (and their types), more and more services should be decentralized and placed at network edge. Even though significant progresses have been made in both academic and industry world, there are still quite some gaps and challenges to improve edge computing systems, especially in resource utilization efficiency and complexity. But most researches on edge computing only focus on some very specific features of edge computing. We proposed a generalized framework of edge computing with services as the core of edge computing in every layer. Based on our framework, we analyzed research works from both academia and industry. According to our analysis, we summarize that the challenges and opportunities lie in resource management, modification of application model, collaboration, security privacy and customization. We hope our framework can be helpful to further improve edge computing eco-systems in real world and attract the community's attention to the challenges and opportunities we identified.

References

1. Zwolenski, M., Weatherill, L.: The digital universe: rich data and the increasing value of the Internet of Things. Austral. J. Telecommun. Digit. Econ. **2**(3), 47 (2014)
2. What is Edge Computing: The Network Edge Explained. https://www.cloudwards.net/what-is-edge-computing/. Accessed 14 May 2019
3. Shi, W., Cao, J., Zhang, Q., Li, Y., Xu, L.: Edge computing: vision and challenges. IEEE IoT J. **3**(5), 637–646 (2016)
4. Yang, S., Li, F., Shen, M., Chen, X., Fu, X., Wang, Y.: Cloudlet placement and task allocation in mobile edge computing. IEEE IoT J. **6**(3), 5853–5863 (2019)
5. Xu, X., et al.: An edge computing-enabled computation offloading method with privacy preservation for internet of connected vehicles. Futur. Gener. Comput. Syst. **96**, 89–100 (2019)
6. Badri, H., Bahreini, T., Grosu, D., Yang, K.: Energy-aware application placement in mobile edge computing: a stochastic optimization approach. IEEE Trans. Parallel Distrib. Syst. **31**(4), 909–922 (2020)
7. Shinkuma, R., Kato, S., Kanbayashi, M.: System design for predictive road-traffic information delivery using edge-cloud computing. In: 15th Annual IEEE Consumer Communications and Networking Conference, CCNC 2018, Las Vegas, pp. 1–6. IEEE (2018)
8. Yang, Y., Wang, K., Zhang, G., Chen, X., Luo, X., Zhou, M.T.: MEETS: maximal energy efficient task scheduling in homogeneous fog networks. IEEE IoT J. **5**(5), 4076–4087 (2018)
9. Wang, L., Jiao, L., Li, J., Gedeon, J., Max, M.: MOERA: mobility-agnostic online resource allocation for edge computing. IEEE Trans. Mob. Comput. **18**(8), 1843–1856 (2019)
10. Ouyang, T., Zhou, Z., Chen, X.: Follow me at the edge: mobility-aware dynamic service placement for mobile edge computing. IEEE J. Sel. Areas Commun. **36**(10), 2333–2345 (2018)
11. Mehran, N., Kimovski, D., Prodan, R.: MAPO: a multi-objective model for IoT application placement in a fog environment. In: ACM International Conference Proceeding Series, pp. 1–8. ACM, New York (2019)
12. He, X., Ren, Z., Shi, C., Fang, J.: A novel load balancing strategy of software-defined cloud/fog networking in the Internet of Vehicles. Chin. Commun. **13**, 140–149 (2016)
13. Li, J., Liang, W., Huang, M., Jia, X.: Reliability-aware network service provisioning in mobile edge-cloud networks. IEEE Trans. Parallel Distrib. Syst. **31**(7), 1545–1558 (2020)
14. Keshtkarjahromi, Y., Xing, Y., Seferoglu, H.: Dynamic heterogeneity-aware coded cooperative computation at the edge. In: 2018 IEEE 26th International Conference on Network Protocols (ICNP), Cambridge, pp. 23–33. IEEE (2018)
15. arXiv:1711.01683. Accessed 01 Aug 2020
16. Ouyang, T., Li, R., Chen, X., Zhou, Z., Tang, X.: Adaptive user-managed service placement for mobile edge computing: an online learning approach. In: IEEE International Conference on Computer Communications, IEEE INFOCOM 2019, Paris, pp. 1468–1476. IEEE (2019)
17. Kaur, K., Garg, S., Aujla, G.S., Kumar, N., Rodrigues, J.J.P.C., Guizani, M.: Edge computing in the industrial Internet of Things environment: software-defined-networks-based edge-cloud interplay. IEEE Commun. Mag. **56**(2), 44–51 (2018)

18. Chen, X., Zhang, J.: When D2D meets cloud: hybrid mobile task offloadings in fog computing. In: IEEE International Conference on Communications, ICC 2017, Paris, pp. 1–6. IEEE (2017)
19. Sahni, Y., Cao, J., Zhang, S.: Edge mesh: a new paradigm to enable distributed intelligence in internet of things. IEEE Access **5**, 16441–16458 (2017)
20. Liu, Y., Yang, C., Jiang, L., Xie, S., Zhang, Y.: Intelligent edge computing for iot-based energy management in smart cities. IEEE Netw. **33**(2), 111–117 (2019)
21. Zamzam, M., Elshabrawy, T., Ashour, M.: Resource management using machine learning in mobile edge computing: a survey. In: 9th International Conference on Intelligent Computing and Information Systems, ICICIS 2019, Cairo, pp. 112–117. IEEE (2019)
22. Yang, T., Hu, Y., Gursoy, M.C., Schmeink, A., Mathar, R.: Deep reinforcement learning based resource allocation in low latency edge computing networks. In: 15th International Symposium on Wireless Communication Systems, ISWCS 2018, Lisbon, pp. 1–5. IEEE (2018)
23. Skirelis, J., Navakauskas, D.: Classifier based gateway for edge computing. In: IEEE 6th Workshop on Advances in Information, Electronic and Electrical Engineering, AIEEE 2018, Vilnius, pp. 1–4. IEEE (2018)
24. Yang, L., Zhang, L., He, Z., Cao, J., Wu, W.: Efficient hybrid data dissemination for edge-assisted automated driving. IEEE IoT J. **7**(1), 148–159 (2020)
25. Yang, L., Liu, B., Cao, J., Sahni, Y., Wang, Z.: Joint computation partitioning and resource allocation for latency sensitive applications in mobile edge clouds. IEEE Trans. Serv. Comput. **1374**, 1–14 (2018)
26. Chen, X., Jiao, L., Li, W., Fu, X.: Efficient multi-user computation offloading for mobile-edge cloud computing. IEEE/ACM Trans. Netw. **24**(5), 2795–2808 (2016)
27. Ma, H., Zhou, Z., Chen, X.: Predictive service placement in mobile edge computing. In: IEEE/CIC International Conference on Communications in China, ICCC 2019, Changchun, pp. 792–797. IEEE (2019)
28. Sahni, Y., Cao, J., Yang, L.: Data-aware task allocation for achieving low latency in collaborative edge computing. IEEE IoT J. **6**(2), 3512–3524 (2019)
29. Zhou, P., Zhang, W., Braud, T., Hui, P., Kangasharju, J.: Enhanced augmented reality applications in vehicle-to-edge networks. In: 22nd Conference on Innovation in Clouds, Internet and Networks and Workshops, ICIN 2019, Paris, pp. 167–174. IEEE (2019)
30. Qian, Y., Hu, L., Chen, J., Guan, X., Hassan, M.M., Alelaiwi, A.: Privacy-aware service placement for mobile edge computing via federated learning. Inf. Sci. **505**, 562–570 (2019)
31. Lu, X., Liao, Y., Lio, P., Hui, P.: Privacy-preserving asynchronous federated learning mechanism for edge network computing. IEEE Access **8**, 48970–48981 (2020)
32. Yuan, J., Li, X.: A multi-source feedback based trust calculation mechanism for edge computing. In: INFOCOM 2018, Honolulu, pp. 819–824. IEEE (2018)
33. Fan, K., Pan, Q., Wang, J., Liu, T., Li, H., Yang, Y.: Cross-domain based data sharing scheme in cooperative edge computing. In: Proceedings of the IEEE International Conference on Edge Computing, (EDGE 2018); World Congress on Services (SERVICES 2018), Seattle, pp. 87–92. IEEE (2018)
34. Deng, X., Liu, J., Wang, L., Zhao, Z.: A trust evaluation system based on reputation data in mobile edge computing network. Peer-to-Peer Netw. Appl. **13**, 1744–1755 (2020). https://doi.org/10.1007/s12083-020-00889-3
35. Gai, K., Qiu, M., Xiong, Z., Liu, M.: Privacy-preserving multi-channel communication in Edge-of-Things. Futur. Gener. Comput. Syst. **85**, 190–200 (2018)
36. Barik, R.K., Dubey, H., Mankodiya, K.: SOA-FOG: secure service-oriented edge computing architecture for smart health big data analytics. In: 2017 IEEE Global Conference on Signal and Information Processing, Montreal, pp. 477–481. IEEE (2018)

37. Li, X., Liu, S., Wu, F., Kumari, S., Rodrigues, J.J.P.C.: Privacy preserving data aggregation scheme for mobile edge computing assisted IoT applications. IEEE IoT J. **6**(3), 4755–4763 (2019)
38. Yousafzai, A., Yaqoob, I., Imran, M., Gani, A., Noor, R.M.: Process migration-based computational offloading framework for IoT-supported mobile edge/cloud computing. IEEE IoT J. **7**(5), 4171–4182 (2019)
39. Wong, W., Zavodovski, A., Zhou, P., Kangasharju, J.: Container deployment strategy for edge networking. In: Proceedings of the 2019 4th Workshop on Middleware for Edge Clouds & Cloudlets, Middleware 2019, Davis, pp. 1–6. ACM (2019)
40. Shi, C., Lakafosis, V., Ammar, M.H., Zegura, E.W.: Serendipity: enabling remote computing among intermittently connected mobile devices. In: Proceedings of 13th ACM International Symposium on MobiHoc, New York, pp. 145–154. ACM (2011)
41. Borgia, E., Bruno, R., Conti, M., Mascitti, D., Passarella, A.: Mobile edge clouds for information-centric IoT services. In: 2016 IEEE Symposium on Computers and Communication, vol. 1, pp. 422–428 (2016)
42. Wang, X., Yang, L.T., Xie, X., Jin, J., Deen, M.J.: A cloud-edge computing framework for cyber-physical-social services. IEEE Commun. **55**(11), 80–85 (2017)
43. Xiao, Y., Noreikis, M., Yla-Jaaiski, A.: QoS-oriented capacity planning for edge computing. In: IEEE International Conference on Communications, pp. 1–6 (2017)
44. Sun, K., Kim, Y.: Network-based VM migration architecture in edge computing. In: ACM International Conference Proceeding Series, Montpellier, pp. 169–172. ACM (2018)
45. Jonathan, A., Ryden, M., Oh, K., Chandra, A., Weissman, J.: Nebula: distributed edge cloud for data intensive computing. IEEE Trans. Parallel Distrib. Syst. **28**(11), 3229–3242 (2017)
46. Sun, Y., Zhou, S., Xu, J.: EMM: energy-aware mobility management for mobile edge computing in ultra dense networks. IEEE J. Sel. Areas Commun. **35**(11), 2637–2646 (2017)
47. Ning, Z., Dong, P., Wang, X., Rodrigues, J.J.P.C., Xia, F.: Deep reinforcement learning for vehicular edge computing: an intelligent offloading system. ACM Trans. Intell. Syst. Technol. **10**(6), 1–24 (2019)
48. Zhao, J., Li, Q., Gong, Y., Zhang, K.: Computation offloading and resource allocation for cloud assisted mobile edge computing in vehicular networks. IEEE Trans. Veh. Technol. **68**(8), 7944–7956 (2019)
49. Gutierrez-Estevez, D.M., Luo, M.: Multi-resource schedulable unit for adaptive application-driven unified resource management in data centers. In: 25th International Telecommunication Networks and Application Conference (ITNAC), Sydney, pp. 261–268. IEEE (2015)
50. Luo, M., Li, L., Chou, W.: ADARM: an application-driven adaptive resource management framework for data centers. In: 2017 IEEE 6th International Conference on AI & Mobile Services (AIMS), Hawaii, pp. 76–84. IEEE (2017)
51. Google Cloud: Cloud IoT Core. https://cloud.google.com/iot-core/. Accessed 11 Aug 2020
52. New Reference Architecture is a Leap Forward for Fog Computing in Cisco Blogs. https://blogs.cisco.com/innovation/new-reference-architecture-is-a-leap-forward-for-fog-computing. Accessed 11 Aug 2020
53. AWS IoT. https://aws.amazon.com/iot/solutions/industrial-iot/?nc1=h_ls. Accessed 11 Aug 2020
54. Edge AI and Azure Stack - Azure Solution Ideas. https://docs.microsoft.com/zh-cn/azure/architecture/solution-ideas/articles/ai-at-the-edge. Accessed 11 Aug 2020
55. Edge Computing Reference Architecture 2.0. http://www.ecconsortium.org/Uploads/file/20190221/1550718911180625.pdf. Accessed 11 Aug 2020

Correction to: Edge Computing – EDGE 2020

Ajay Katangur, Shih-Chun Lin, Jinpeng Wei⊙, Shuhui Yang,
and Liang-Jie Zhang ⊙

Correction to:
A. Katangur et al. (Eds.): *Edge Computing – EDGE 2020*,
LNCS 12407, https://doi.org/10.1007/978-3-030-59824-2

In the original version of this book, the affiliation on the imprint page of the second editor and on the organizing pages of the second program chair member Shih-Chun Lin was not correct.

It should be read as follows:

Shih-Chun Lin North Carolina State University, USA.

This has been now corrected.

The updated version of the book can be found at
https://doi.org/10.1007/978-3-030-59824-2

© Springer Nature Switzerland AG 2020
A. Katangur et al. (Eds.): EDGE 2020, LNCS 12407, p. C1, 2020.
https://doi.org/10.1007/978-3-030-59824-2_11

Author Index

Printed in the United States
By Bookmasters